BRITISH ENGLISH COLLECTION

ENGLISH AFRIKAANS

THEME-BASED DICTIONARY

Contains over 3000 commonly used words

T&P BOOKS PUBLISHING

Theme-based dictionary British English-Afrikaans - 3000 words
British English collection

By Andrey Taranov

T&P Books vocabularies are intended for helping you learn, memorize and review foreign words. The dictionary is divided into themes, covering all major spheres of everyday activities, business, science, culture, etc.

The process of learning words using T&P Books' theme-based dictionaries gives you the following advantages:

- Correctly grouped source information predetermines success at subsequent stages of word memorization
- Availability of words derived from the same root allowing memorization of word units (rather than separate words)
- Small units of words facilitate the process of establishing associative links needed for consolidation of vocabulary
- Level of language knowledge can be estimated by the number of learned words

T&P Books Publishing
www.tpbooks.com

ISBN: 978-1-78716-510-6

This book is also available in E-book formats.
Please visit www.tpbooks.com or the major online bookstores.

AFRIKAANS THEME-BASED DICTIONARY
British English collection

T&P Books vocabularies are intended to help you learn, memorize, and review foreign words. The vocabulary contains over 3000 commonly used words arranged thematically.

- Vocabulary contains the most commonly used words
- Recommended as an addition to any language course
- Meets the needs of beginners and advanced learners of foreign languages
- Convenient for daily use, revision sessions, and self-testing activities
- Allows you to assess your vocabulary

Special features of the vocabulary

- Words are organized according to their meaning, not alphabetically
- Words are presented in three columns to facilitate the reviewing and self-testing processes
- Words in groups are divided into small blocks to facilitate the learning process
- The vocabulary offers a convenient and simple transcription of each foreign word

The vocabulary has 101 topics including:

Basic Concepts, Numbers, Colors, Months, Seasons, Units of Measurement, Clothing & Accessories, Food & Nutrition, Restaurant, Family Members, Relatives, Character, Feelings, Emotions, Diseases, City, Town, Sightseeing, Shopping, Money, House, Home, Office, Working in the Office, Import & Export, Marketing, Job Search, Sports, Education, Computer, Internet, Tools, Nature, Countries, Nationalities and more ...

TABLE OF CONTENTS

PRONUNCIATION GUIDE

T&P phonetic alphabet	Afrikaans example	English example
[a]	land	shorter than in ask
[ã]	straat	calf, palm
[æ]	hout	chess, man
[o], [ɔ]	Australië	drop, baught
[e]	metaal	elm, medal
[ɛ]	aanlê	man, bad
[ə]	filter	driver, teacher
[ɪ]	uur	big, America
[i]	billik	shorter than in feet
[ī]	naïef	tree, big
[o]	koppie	pod, John
[ø]	akteur	eternal, church
[œ]	fluit	German Hölle
[u]	hulle	book
[ʊ]	hout	good, booklet
[b]	bakker	baby, book
[d]	donder	day, doctor
[f]	navraag	face, food
[g]	burger	game, gold
[h]	driehoek	home, have
[j]	byvoeg	yes, New York
[k]	kamera	clock, kiss
[l]	loon	lace, people
[m]	môre	magic, milk
[n]	neef	sang, thing
[p]	pyp	pencil, private
[r]	rigting	rice, radio
[s]	oplos	city, boss
[t]	lood, tenk	tourist, trip
[v]	bewaar	very, river
[w]	oorwinnaar	vase, winter
[z]	zoem	zebra, please
[dʒ]	enjin	joke, general
[ʃ]	artisjok	machine, shark
[ŋ]	kans	English, ring
[ʧ]	tjek	church, French
[ʒ]	beige	forge, pleasure
[x]	agent	as in Scots 'loch'

ABBREVIATIONS
used in the dictionary

English abbreviations

ab.	-	about
adj	-	adjective
adv	-	adverb
anim.	-	animate
as adj	-	attributive noun used as adjective
e.g.	-	for example
etc.	-	et cetera
fam.	-	familiar
fem.	-	feminine
form.	-	formal
inanim.	-	inanimate
masc.	-	masculine
math	-	mathematics
mil.	-	military
n	-	noun
pl	-	plural
pron.	-	pronoun
sb	-	somebody
sing.	-	singular
sth	-	something
v aux	-	auxiliary verb
vi	-	intransitive verb
vi, vt	-	intransitive, transitive verb
vt	-	transitive verb

BASIC CONCEPTS

1. Pronouns

I, me	**ek, my**	[ɛk], [maj]
you	**jy**	[jaj]
he	**hy**	[haj]
she	**sy**	[saj]
it	**dit**	[dit]
we	**ons**	[ɔŋs]
you (to a group)	**julle**	[jullə]
you (polite, sing.)	**u**	[u]
you (polite, pl)	**u**	[u]
they	**hulle**	[hullə]

2. Greetings. Salutations

Hello! (fam.)	**Hallo!**	[hallo!]
Hello! (form.)	**Hallo!**	[hallo!]
Good morning!	**Goeie môre!**	[χuje mɔrə!]
Good afternoon!	**Goeiemiddag!**	[χuje·middaχ!]
Good evening!	**Goeienaand!**	[χuje·nãnt!]
to say hello	**dagsê**	[daχsɛ:]
Hi! (hello)	**Hallo!**	[hallo!]
greeting (n)	**groet**	[χrut]
to greet (vt)	**groet**	[χrut]
How are you?	**Hoe gaan dit?**	[hu χãn dit?]
What's new?	**Hoe gaan dit?**	[hu χãn dit?]
Goodbye!	**Totsiens!**	[totsiŋs!]
Bye!	**Koebaai!**	[kubãi!]
See you soon!	**Totsiens!**	[totsiŋs!]
Farewell!	**Totsiens!**	[totsiŋs!]
Farewell! (to a friend)	**Mooi loop!**	[moj loəp!]
Farewell! (form.)	**Vaarwel!**	[fãrwel!]
to say goodbye	**afskeid neem**	[afskæjt neəm]
Cheers!	**Koebaai!**	[kubãi!]
Thank you! Cheers!	**Dankie!**	[danki!]
Thank you very much!	**Baie dankie!**	[baje danki!]
My pleasure!	**Plesier**	[plesir]
Don't mention it!	**Plesier!**	[plesir!]
It was nothing	**Plesier**	[plesir]
Excuse me! (fam.)	**Ekskuus!**	[ɛkskɪs!]
Excuse me! (form.)	**Verskoon my!**	[ferskoən maj!]

to excuse (forgive)	verskoon	[ferskoən]
to apologize (vi)	verskoning vra	[ferskoniŋ fra]
My apologies	Verskoning	[ferskoniŋ]
I'm sorry!	Ek is jammer!	[ɛk is jammər!]
to forgive (vt)	vergewe	[ferχeve]
It's okay! (that's all right)	Maak nie saak nie!	[māk ni sāk ni!]
please (adv)	asseblief	[asseblif]

Don't forget!	Vergeet dit nie!	[ferχeet dit ni!]
Certainly!	Beslis!	[beslis!]
Of course not!	Natuurlik nie!	[natɪrlik ni!]
Okay! (I agree)	OK!	[okej!]
That's enough!	Dis genoeg!	[dis χenuχ!]

3. Questions

Who?	Wie?	[vi?]
What?	Wat?	[vat?]
Where? (at, in)	Waar?	[vār?]
Where (to)?	Waarheen?	[vārheən?]
From where?	Waarvandaan?	[vārfandān?]
When?	Wanneer?	[vanneər?]
Why? (What for?)	Hoekom?	[hukom?]
Why? (~ are you crying?)	Hoekom?	[hukom?]

What for?	Vir wat?	[fir vat?]
How? (in what way)	Hoe?	[hu?]
What? (What kind of ...?)	Watter?	[vattər?]
Which?	Watter een?	[vattər eən?]

To whom?	Vir wie?	[fir vi?]
About whom?	Oor wie?	[oər vi?]
About what?	Oor wat?	[oər vat?]
With whom?	Met wie?	[met vi?]
How many? How much?	Hoeveel?	[hufeəl?]

4. Prepositions

with (accompanied by)	met	[met]
without	sonder	[sondər]
to (indicating direction)	na	[na]
about (talking ~ ...)	oor	[oər]
before (in time)	voor	[foər]
in front of ...	voor ...	[foər ...]

under (beneath, below)	onder	[ondər]
above (over)	oor	[oər]
on (atop)	op	[op]
from (off, out of)	uit	[œit]
of (made from)	van	[fan]
in (e.g. ~ ten minutes)	oor	[oər]
over (across the top of)	oor	[oər]

5. Function words. Adverbs. Part 1

Where? (at, in)	Waar?	[vãr?]
here (adv)	hier	[hir]
there (adv)	daar	[dãr]
somewhere (to be)	êrens	[ærɛŋs]
nowhere (not anywhere)	nêrens	[nærɛŋs]
by (near, beside)	by	[baj]
by the window	by	[baj]
Where (to)?	Waarheen?	[vãrheən?]
here (e.g. come ~!)	hier	[hir]
there (e.g. to go ~)	soontoe	[soentu]
from here (adv)	hiervandaan	[hirfandãn]
from there (adv)	daarvandaan	[dãrfandãn]
close (adv)	naby	[nabaj]
far (adv)	ver	[fer]
near (e.g. ~ Paris)	naby	[nabaj]
nearby (adv)	naby	[nabaj]
not far (adv)	nie ver nie	[ni fər ni]
left (adj)	linker-	[linkər-]
on the left	op linkerhand	[op linkərhant]
to the left	na links	[na links]
right (adj)	regter	[reχtər]
on the right	op regterhand	[op reχtərhant]
to the right	na regs	[na reχs]
in front (adv)	voor	[foər]
front (as adj)	voorste	[foərstə]
ahead (the kids ran ~)	vooruit	[foərœit]
behind (adv)	agter	[aχtər]
from behind	van agter	[fan aχtər]
back (towards the rear)	agtertoe	[aχtərtu]
middle	middel	[middəl]
in the middle	in die middel	[in di middəl]
at the side	op die sykant	[op di sajkant]
everywhere (adv)	orals	[orals]
around (in all directions)	orals rond	[orals ront]
from inside	van binne	[fan binnə]
somewhere (to go)	êrens	[ærɛŋs]
straight (directly)	reguit	[reχœit]
back (e.g. come ~)	terug	[teruχ]
from anywhere	êrens vandaan	[ærɛŋs fandãn]
from somewhere	êrens vandaan	[ærɛŋs fandãn]

firstly (adv)	in die eerste plek	[in di eǝrstǝ plek]
secondly (adv)	in die tweede plek	[in di tweǝdǝ plek]
thirdly (adv)	in die derde plek	[in di derdǝ plek]

suddenly (adv)	skielik	[skilik]
at first (in the beginning)	aan die begin	[ān di beχin]
for the first time	vir die eerste keer	[fir di eǝrstǝ keǝr]
long before ...	lank voordat ...	[lank foǝrdat ...]
anew (over again)	opnuut	[opnɪt]
for good (adv)	vir goed	[fir χut]

never (adv)	nooit	[nojt]
again (adv)	weer	[veǝr]
now (adv)	nou	[næʊ]
often (adv)	dikwels	[dikwɛls]
then (adv)	toe	[tu]
urgently (quickly)	dringend	[driŋǝn]
usually (adv)	gewoonlik	[χevoǝnlik]

by the way, ...	terloops, ...	[terloǝps], [...]
possible (that is ~)	moontlik	[moentlik]
probably (adv)	waarskynlik	[vārskajnlik]
maybe (adv)	dalk	[dalk]
besides ...	trouens...	[træʊɛŋs...]
that's why ...	dis hoekom ...	[dis hukom ...]
in spite of ...	ondanks ...	[ondanks ...]
thanks to ...	danksy ...	[danksaj ...]

what (pron.)	wat	[vat]
that (conj.)	dat	[dat]
something	iets	[its]
anything (something)	iets	[its]
nothing	niks	[niks]

who (pron.)	wie	[vi]
someone	iemand	[imant]
somebody	iemand	[imant]

nobody	niemand	[nimant]
nowhere (a voyage to ~)	nêrens	[nærɛŋs]
nobody's	niemand se	[nimant sǝ]
somebody's	iemand se	[imant sǝ]

so (I'm ~ glad)	so	[so]
also (as well)	ook	[oǝk]
too (as well)	ook	[oǝk]

6. Function words. Adverbs. Part 2

| Why? | Waarom? | [vārom?] |
| because ... | omdat ... | [omdat ...] |

| and | en | [ɛn] |
| or | of | [of] |

| but | maar | [mãr] |
| for (e.g. ~ me) | vir | [fir] |

too (excessively)	te	[te]
only (exclusively)	net	[net]
exactly (adv)	presies	[presis]
about (more or less)	ongeveer	[onχəfeər]

approximately (adv)	ongeveer	[onχəfeər]
approximate (adj)	geraamde	[χerãmdə]
almost (adv)	amper	[ampər]
the rest	die res	[di res]

the other (second)	die ander	[di andər]
other (different)	ander	[andər]
each (adj)	elke	[ɛlkə]
any (no matter which)	enige	[ɛniχə]
many (adv)	baie	[bajə]
much (adv)	baie	[bajə]
many people	baie mense	[bajə mɛŋsə]
all (everyone)	almal	[almal]

in return for …	in ruil vir…	[in rœil fir…]
in exchange (adv)	as vergoeding	[as ferχudiŋ]
by hand (made)	met die hand	[met di hant]
hardly (negative opinion)	skaars	[skãrs]

probably (adv)	waarskynlik	[vãrskajnlik]
on purpose (intentionally)	opsetlik	[opsetlik]
by accident (adv)	toevallig	[tufalləχ]

very (adv)	baie	[bajə]
for example (adv)	byvoorbeeld	[bajfoərbeəlt]
between	tussen	[tussən]
among	tussen	[tussən]
so much (such a lot)	so baie	[so bajə]
especially (adv)	veral	[feral]

NUMBERS. MISCELLANEOUS

7. Cardinal numbers. Part 1

0 zero	nul	[nul]
1 one	een	[eən]
2 two	twee	[tweə]
3 three	drie	[dri]
4 four	vier	[fir]
5 five	vyf	[fajf]
6 six	ses	[ses]
7 seven	sewe	[sevə]
8 eight	ag	[aχ]
9 nine	nege	[neχə]
10 ten	tien	[tin]
11 eleven	elf	[ɛlf]
12 twelve	twaalf	[twālf]
13 thirteen	dertien	[dertin]
14 fourteen	veertien	[feərtin]
15 fifteen	vyftien	[fajftin]
16 sixteen	sestien	[sestin]
17 seventeen	sewetien	[sevətin]
18 eighteen	agtien	[aχtin]
19 nineteen	negetien	[neχetin]
20 twenty	twintig	[twintəχ]
21 twenty-one	een-en-twintig	[eən-en-twintəχ]
22 twenty-two	twee-en-twintig	[tweə-en-twintəχ]
23 twenty-three	drie-en-twintig	[dri-en-twintəχ]
30 thirty	dertig	[dertəχ]
31 thirty-one	een-en-dertig	[eən-en-dertəχ]
32 thirty-two	twee-en-dertig	[tweə-en-dertəχ]
33 thirty-three	drie-en-dertig	[dri-en-dertəχ]
40 forty	veertig	[feərtəχ]
41 forty-one	een-en-veertig	[eən-en-feərtəχ]
42 forty-two	twee-en-veertig	[tweə-en-feərtəχ]
43 forty-three	vier-en-veertig	[fir-en-feərtəχ]
50 fifty	vyftig	[fajftəχ]
51 fifty-one	een-en-vyftig	[eən-en-fajftəχ]
52 fifty-two	twee-en-vyftig	[tweə-en-fajftəχ]
53 fifty-three	drie-en-vyftig	[dri-en-fajftəχ]
60 sixty	sestig	[sestəχ]
61 sixty-one	een-en-sestig	[eən-en-sestəχ]

| 62 sixty-two | twee-en-sestig | [twee-en-sestəχ] |
| 63 sixty-three | drie-en-sestig | [dri-en-sestəχ] |

70 seventy	sewentig	[seventəχ]
71 seventy-one	een-en-sewentig	[een-en-seventəχ]
72 seventy-two	twee-en-sewentig	[twee-en-seventəχ]
73 seventy-three	drie-en-sewentig	[dri-en-seventəχ]

80 eighty	tagtig	[taχtəχ]
81 eighty-one	een-en-tagtig	[een-en-taχtəχ]
82 eighty-two	twee-en-tagtig	[twee-en-taχtəχ]
83 eighty-three	drie-en-tagtig	[dri-en-taχtəχ]

90 ninety	negentig	[neχentəχ]
91 ninety-one	een-en-negentig	[een-en-neχentəχ]
92 ninety-two	twee-en-negentig	[twee-en-neχentəχ]
93 ninety-three	drie-en-negentig	[dri-en-neχentəχ]

8. Cardinal numbers. Part 2

100 one hundred	honderd	[hondərt]
200 two hundred	tweehonderd	[twee·hondərt]
300 three hundred	driehonderd	[dri·hondərt]
400 four hundred	vierhonderd	[fir·hondərt]
500 five hundred	vyfhonderd	[fajf·hondərt]

600 six hundred	seshonderd	[ses·hondərt]
700 seven hundred	sewehonderd	[sewe·hondərt]
800 eight hundred	aghonderd	[aχ·hondərt]
900 nine hundred	negehonderd	[neχe·hondərt]

1000 one thousand	duisend	[dœisent]
2000 two thousand	tweeduisend	[twee·dœisent]
3000 three thousand	drieduisend	[dri·dœisent]
10000 ten thousand	tienduisend	[tin·dœisent]
one hundred thousand	honderdduisend	[hondərt·dajsent]
million	miljoen	[miljun]
billion	miljard	[miljart]

9. Ordinal numbers

first (adj)	eerste	[eerstə]
second (adj)	tweede	[tweedə]
third (adj)	derde	[derdə]
fourth (adj)	vierde	[firdə]
fifth (adj)	vyfde	[fajfdə]

sixth (adj)	sesde	[sesdə]
seventh (adj)	sewende	[sewendə]
eighth (adj)	agste	[aχstə]
ninth (adj)	negende	[neχendə]
tenth (adj)	tiende	[tində]

COLORS. UNITS OF MEASUREMENT

10. Colours

colour	kleur	[kløər]
shade (tint)	skakering	[skakeriŋ]
hue	tint	[tint]
rainbow	reënboog	[rɛɛn·boəχ]

white (adj)	wit	[vit]
black (adj)	swart	[swart]
grey (adj)	grys	[χrajs]

green (adj)	groen	[χrun]
yellow (adj)	geel	[χeəl]
red (adj)	rooi	[roj]

blue (adj)	blou	[blæʊ]
light blue (adj)	ligblou	[liχ·blæʊ]
pink (adj)	pienk	[pink]
orange (adj)	oranje	[oranje]
violet (adj)	pers	[pers]
brown (adj)	bruin	[brœin]

golden (adj)	goue	[χæʊə]
silvery (adj)	silweragtig	[silweraχtəχ]

beige (adj)	beige	[bɛ:iʒ]
cream (adj)	roomkleurig	[roəm·kløərəχ]
turquoise (adj)	turkoois	[turkojs]
cherry red (adj)	kersierooi	[kersi·roj]
lilac (adj)	lila	[lila]
crimson (adj)	karmosyn	[karmosajn]

light (adj)	lig	[liχ]
dark (adj)	donker	[donkər]
bright, vivid (adj)	helder	[hɛldər]

coloured (pencils)	kleurig	[kløərəχ]
colour (e.g. ~ film)	kleur	[kløər]
black-and-white (adj)	swart-wit	[swart-wit]
plain (one-coloured)	effe	[ɛffə]
multicoloured (adj)	veelkleurig	[feəlkløərəχ]

11. Units of measurement

weight	gewig	[χevəχ]
length	lengte	[leŋtə]

width	breedte	[breədtə]
height	hoogte	[hoəχtə]
depth	diepte	[diptə]
volume	volume	[folumə]
area	area	[areɑ]

gram	gram	[χram]
milligram	milligram	[milliχram]
kilogram	kilogram	[kiloχram]
ton	ton	[ton]
pound	pond	[pont]
ounce	ons	[ɔŋs]

metre	meter	[metər]
millimetre	millimeter	[millimetər]
centimetre	sentimeter	[sentimetər]
kilometre	kilometer	[kilometər]
mile	myl	[majl]

inch	duim	[dœim]
foot	voet	[fut]
yard	jaart	[jãrt]

| square metre | vierkante meter | [firkantə metər] |
| hectare | hektaar | [hektãr] |

litre	liter	[litər]
degree	graad	[χrãt]
volt	volt	[folt]
ampere	ampère	[ampɛ:r]
horsepower	perdekrag	[perdə·kraχ]

quantity	hoeveelheid	[hufeəlhæjt]
half	helfte	[hɛlftə]
dozen	dosyn	[dosajn]
piece (item)	stuk	[stuk]

| size | grootte | [χroəttə] |
| scale (map ~) | skaal | [skãl] |

minimal (adj)	minimaal	[minimãl]
the smallest (adj)	die kleinste	[di klæjnstə]
medium (adj)	medium	[medium]
maximal (adj)	maksimaal	[maksimãl]
the largest (adj)	die grootste	[di χroətstə]

12. Containers

canning jar (glass ~)	glaspot	[χlas·pot]
tin, can	blikkie	[blikki]
bucket	emmer	[ɛmmər]
barrel	drom	[drom]
wash basin (e.g., plastic ~)	wasbak	[vas·bak]
tank (100L water ~)	tenk	[tɛnk]

hip flask	heupfles	[høəp·fles]
jerrycan	petrolblik	[petrol·blik]
tank (e.g., tank car)	tenk	[tɛnk]

mug	beker	[bekər]
cup (of coffee, etc.)	koppie	[koppi]
saucer	piering	[piriŋ]
glass (tumbler)	glas	[χlas]
wine glass	wynglas	[vajn·χlas]
stock pot (soup pot)	soppot	[sop·pot]

| bottle (~ of wine) | bottel | [bottəl] |
| neck (of the bottle, etc.) | nek | [nek] |

carafe (decanter)	kraffie	[kraffi]
pitcher	kruik	[krœik]
vessel (container)	houer	[hæʋər]
pot (crock, stoneware ~)	pot	[pot]
vase	vaas	[fãs]

bottle (perfume ~)	bottel	[bottəl]
vial, small bottle	botteltjie	[bottɛlki]
tube (of toothpaste)	buisie	[bœisi]

sack (bag)	sak	[sak]
bag (paper ~, plastic ~)	sak	[sak]
packet (of cigarettes, etc.)	pakkie	[pakki]

box (e.g. shoebox)	kartondoos	[karton·doəs]
crate	krat	[krat]
basket	mandjie	[mandʒi]

MAIN VERBS

13. The most important verbs. Part 1

to advise (vt)	aanraai	[ānrāi]
to agree (say yes)	saamstem	[sāmstem]
to answer (vi, vt)	antwoord	[antwoərt]
to apologize (vi)	verskoning vra	[ferskoniŋ fra]
to arrive (vi)	aankom	[ānkom]
to ask (~ oneself)	vra	[fra]
to ask (~ sb to do sth)	vra	[fra]
to be (vi)	wees	[veəs]
to be afraid	bang wees	[baŋ veəs]
to be hungry	honger wees	[honər veəs]
to be interested in ...	belangstel in ...	[belaŋstəl in ...]
to be needed	nodig wees	[nodəχ veəs]
to be surprised	verbaas wees	[ferbās veəs]
to be thirsty	dors wees	[dors veəs]
to begin (vt)	begin	[beχin]
to belong to ...	behoort aan ...	[behoərt ān ...]
to boast (vi)	spog	[spoχ]
to break (split into pieces)	breek	[breək]
to call (~ for help)	roep	[rup]
can (v aux)	kan	[kan]
to catch (vt)	vang	[faŋ]
to change (vt)	verander	[ferandər]
to choose (select)	kies	[kis]
to come down (the stairs)	afkom	[afkom]
to compare (vt)	vergelyk	[ferχəlajk]
to complain (vi, vt)	kla	[kla]
to confuse (mix up)	verwar	[ferwar]
to continue (vt)	aangaan	[ānχān]
to control (vt)	kontroleer	[kontroleər]
to cook (dinner)	kook	[koək]
to cost (vt)	kos	[kos]
to count (add up)	tel	[təl]
to count on ...	reken op ...	[reken op ...]
to create (vt)	skep	[skep]
to cry (weep)	huil	[hœil]

14. The most important verbs. Part 2

to deceive (vi, vt)	bedrieg	[bedrəχ]
to decorate (tree, street)	versier	[fersir]

to defend (a country, etc.)	verdedig	[ferdedəχ]
to demand (request firmly)	eis	[æjs]
to dig (vt)	grawe	[χravə]

to discuss (vt)	bespreek	[bespreek]
to do (vt)	doen	[dun]
to doubt (have doubts)	twyfel	[twajfəl]
to drop (let fall)	laat val	[lāt fal]
to enter (room, house, etc.)	binnegaan	[binnəχān]

to excuse (forgive)	verskoon	[ferskoən]
to exist (vi)	bestaan	[bestān]
to expect (foresee)	voorsien	[foərsin]
to explain (vt)	verduidelik	[ferdœidəlik]
to fall (vi)	val	[fal]

to fancy (vt)	hou van	[hæʊ fan]
to find (vt)	vind	[fint]
to finish (vt)	klaarmaak	[klārmāk]
to fly (vi)	vlieg	[fliχ]
to follow ... (come after)	volg ...	[folχ ...]

to forget (vi, vt)	vergeet	[ferχeət]
to forgive (vt)	vergewe	[ferχevə]
to give (vt)	gee	[χeə]
to go (on foot)	gaan	[χān]

to go for a swim	gaan swem	[χān swem]
to go out (for dinner, etc.)	uitgaan	[œitχān]
to guess (the answer)	raai	[rāi]

to have (vt)	hê	[hɛ:]
to have breakfast	ontbyt	[ontbajt]
to have dinner	aandete gebruik	[āndetə χebrœik]
to have lunch	gaan eet	[χān eət]
to hear (vt)	hoor	[hoər]

to help (vt)	help	[hɛlp]
to hide (vt)	wegsteek	[veχsteək]
to hope (vi, vt)	hoop	[hoəp]
to hunt (vi, vt)	jag	[jaχ]
to hurry (vi)	opskud	[opskut]

15. The most important verbs. Part 3

to inform (vt)	in kennis stel	[in kɛnnis stəl]
to insist (vi, vt)	aandring	[āndriŋ]
to insult (vt)	beledig	[beledəχ]
to invite (vt)	uitnooi	[œitnoj]
to joke (vi)	grappies maak	[χrappis māk]

to keep (vt)	bewaar	[bevār]
to keep silent	stilbly	[stilblaj]
to kill (vt)	doodmaak	[doədmāk]

to know (sb)	ken	[ken]
to know (sth)	weet	[veət]
to laugh (vi)	lag	[laχ]

to liberate (city, etc.)	bevry	[befraj]
to look for ... (search)	soek ...	[suk ...]
to love (sb)	liefhê	[lifhɛ:]
to manage, to run	beheer	[beheər]

to mean (signify)	beteken	[betekən]
to mention (talk about)	verwys na	[ferwajs na]
to miss (school, etc.)	bank	[bank]
to notice (see)	raaksien	[rãksin]
to object (vi, vt)	beswaar maak	[beswãr mãk]

to observe (see)	waarneem	[vãrneəm]
to open (vt)	oopmaak	[oəpmãk]
to order (meal, etc.)	bestel	[bestəl]
to order (mil.)	beveel	[befeəl]
to own (possess)	besit	[besit]

to participate (vi)	deelneem	[deəlneəm]
to pay (vi, vt)	betaal	[betãl]
to permit (vt)	toestaan	[tustãn]
to plan (vt)	beplan	[beplan]
to play (children)	speel	[speəl]

to pray (vi, vt)	bid	[bit]
to prefer (vt)	verkies	[ferkis]
to promise (vt)	beloof	[beloəf]
to pronounce (vt)	uitspreek	[œitspreək]
to propose (vt)	voorstel	[foərstəl]
to punish (vt)	straf	[straf]

16. The most important verbs. Part 4

to read (vi, vt)	lees	[leəs]
to recommend (vt)	aanbeveel	[ãnbefeəl]
to refuse (vi, vt)	weier	[væejer]
to regret (be sorry)	jammer wees	[jammər veəs]
to rent (sth from sb)	huur	[hɪr]

to repeat (say again)	herhaal	[herhãl]
to reserve, to book	bespreek	[bespreək]
to run (vi)	hardloop	[hardloəp]
to save (rescue)	red	[ret]

to say (~ thank you)	sê	[sɛ:]
to scold (vt)	uitvaar teen	[œitfãr teən]
to see (vt)	sien	[sin]
to sell (vt)	verkoop	[ferkoəp]

to send (vt)	stuur	[stɪr]
to shoot (vi)	skiet	[skit]

to shout (vi)	skreeu	[skriʊ]
to show (vt)	wys	[vajs]
to sign (document)	teken	[tekən]

to sit down (vi)	gaan sit	[χān sit]
to smile (vi)	glimlag	[χlimlaχ]
to speak (vi, vt)	praat	[prāt]
to steal (money, etc.)	steel	[steəl]
to stop (for pause, etc.)	stilhou	[stilhæʊ]

to stop (please ~ calling me)	ophou	[ophæʊ]
to study (vt)	studeer	[studeər]
to swim (vi)	swem	[swem]
to take (vt)	vat	[fat]
to think (vi, vt)	dink	[dink]

to threaten (vt)	dreig	[dræjχ]
to touch (with hands)	aanraak	[ānrāk]
to translate (vt)	vertaal	[fertāl]
to trust (vt)	vertrou	[fertræʊ]
to try (attempt)	probeer	[probeər]

to turn (e.g., ~ left)	draai	[drāi]
to underestimate (vt)	onderskat	[ondərskat]
to understand (vt)	verstaan	[ferstān]
to unite (vt)	verenig	[ferenəχ]
to wait (vt)	wag	[vaχ]

to want (wish, desire)	wil	[vil]
to warn (vt)	waarsku	[vārskuʆ]
to work (vi)	werk	[verk]
to write (vt)	skryf	[skrajf]
to write down	opskryf	[opskrajf]

TIME. CALENDAR

17. Weekdays

Monday	**Maandag**	[mãndaχ]
Tuesday	**Dinsdag**	[dinsdaχ]
Wednesday	**Woensdag**	[voɛŋsdaχ]
Thursday	**Donderdag**	[dondərdaχ]
Friday	**Vrydag**	[frajdaχ]
Saturday	**Saterdag**	[satərdaχ]
Sunday	**Sondag**	[sondaχ]
today (adv)	**vandag**	[fandaχ]
tomorrow (adv)	**môre**	[mɔrə]
the day after tomorrow	**oormôre**	[oərmɔrə]
yesterday (adv)	**gister**	[χistər]
the day before yesterday	**eergister**	[eərχistər]
day	**dag**	[daχ]
working day	**werksdag**	[verks·daχ]
public holiday	**openbare vakansiedag**	[openbarə fakaŋsi·daχ]
day off	**verlofdag**	[ferlofdaχ]
weekend	**naweek**	[naveək]
all day long	**die hele dag**	[di helə daχ]
the next day (adv)	**die volgende dag**	[di folχendə daχ]
two days ago	**twee dae gelede**	[tweə daə χeledə]
the day before	**die dag voor**	[di daχ foər]
daily (adj)	**daeliks**	[daəliks]
every day (adv)	**elke dag**	[ɛlkə daχ]
week	**week**	[veək]
last week (adv)	**laas week**	[lãs veək]
next week (adv)	**volgende week**	[folχendə veək]
weekly (adj)	**weekliks**	[veəkliks]
every week (adv)	**weekliks**	[veəkliks]
every Tuesday	**elke Dinsdag**	[ɛlkə dinsdaχ]

18. Hours. Day and night

morning	**oggend**	[oχent]
in the morning	**soggens**	[soχɛŋs]
noon, midday	**middag**	[middaχ]
in the afternoon	**in die namiddag**	[in di namiddaχ]
evening	**aand**	[ãnt]
in the evening	**saans**	[sãŋs]
night	**nag**	[naχ]

| at night | snags | [snaχs] |
| midnight | middernaġ | [middərnaχ] |

second	sekonde	[sekondə]
minute	minuut	[minɪt]
hour	uur	[ɪr]
half an hour	n halfuur	[n halfɪr]
fifteen minutes	vyftien minute	[fajftin minutə]
24 hours	24 ure	[fir-en-twintəχ urə]

sunrise	sonop	[son·op]
dawn	daeraad	[daerãt]
early morning	elke oggend	[ɛlkə oχent]
sunset	sononder	[son·ondər]

early in the morning	vroegdag	[fruχdaχ]
this morning	vanmôre	[fanmɔrə]
tomorrow morning	môreoggend	[mɔrə·oχent]

this afternoon	vanmiddag	[fanmiddaχ]
in the afternoon	in die namiddag	[in di namiddaχ]
tomorrow afternoon	môremiddag	[mɔrə·middaχ]

| tonight (this evening) | vanaand | [fanãnt] |
| tomorrow night | môreaand | [mɔrə·ãnt] |

at 3 o'clock sharp	klokslag 3 uur	[klokslaχ dri ɪr]
about 4 o'clock	omstreeks 4 uur	[omstreəks fir ɪr]
by 12 o'clock	teen 12 uur	[teən twalf ɪr]
in 20 minutes	oor twintig minute	[oər twintəχ minutə]
on time (adv)	betyds	[betajds]

a quarter to …	kwart voor …	[kwart foər …]
every 15 minutes	elke 15 minute	[ɛlkə fajftin minutə]
round the clock	24 uur per dag	[fir-en-twintəχ pər daχ]

19. Months. Seasons

January	Januarie	[januari]
February	Februarie	[februari]
March	Maart	[mãrt]
April	April	[april]
May	Mei	[mæj]
June	Junie	[juni]

July	Julie	[juli]
August	Augustus	[ɔuχustus]
September	September	[septembər]
October	Oktober	[oktobər]
November	November	[nofembər]
December	Desember	[desembər]

| spring | lente | [lentə] |
| in spring | in die lente | [in di lentə] |

spring (as adj)	lente-	[lente-]
summer	somer	[somər]
in summer	in die somer	[in di somər]
summer (as adj)	somerse	[somersə]

autumn	herfs	[herfs]
in autumn	in die herfs	[in di herfs]
autumn (as adj)	herfsagtige	[herfsaχtiχə]

winter	winter	[vintər]
in winter	in die winter	[in di vintər]
winter (as adj)	winter-	[vintər-]

month	maand	[mānt]
this month	hierdie maand	[hirdi mānt]
next month	volgende maand	[folχendə mānt]
last month	laasmaand	[lāsmānt]

| in 2 months (2 months later) | oor twe maande | [oər twə māndə] |
| the whole month | die hele maand | [di helə mānt] |

monthly (~ magazine)	maandeliks	[māndəliks]
monthly (adv)	maandeliks	[māndəliks]
every month	elke maand	[ɛlkə mānt]

year	jaar	[jār]
this year	hierdie jaar	[hirdi jār]
next year	volgende jaar	[folχendə jār]
last year	laasjaar	[lāʃār]

| in two years | binne twee jaar | [binnə tweə jār] |
| the whole year | die hele jaar | [di helə jār] |

every year	elke jaar	[ɛlkə jār]
annual (adj)	jaarliks	[jārliks]
annually (adv)	jaarliks	[jārliks]
4 times a year	4 keer per jaar	[fir keər pər jār]

date (e.g. today's ~)	datum	[datum]
date (e.g. ~ of birth)	datum	[datum]
calendar	kalender	[kalendər]

six months	ses maande	[ses māndə]
season (summer, etc.)	seisoen	[sæjsun]
century	eeu	[iʊ]

TRAVEL. HOTEL

20. Trip. Travel

tourism, travel	**toerisme**	[turismə]
tourist	**toeris**	[turis]
trip, voyage	**reis**	[ræjs]
adventure	**avontuur**	[afontɪr]
trip, journey	**reis**	[ræjs]
holiday	**vakansie**	[fakaŋsi]
to be on holiday	**met vakansie wees**	[met fakaŋsi veəs]
rest	**rus**	[rus]
train	**trein**	[træjn]
by train	**per trein**	[pər træjn]
aeroplane	**vliegtuig**	[fliχtœiχ]
by aeroplane	**per vliegtuig**	[pər fliχtœiχ]
by car	**per motor**	[pər motor]
by ship	**per skip**	[pər skip]
luggage	**bagasie**	[baχasi]
suitcase	**tas**	[tas]
luggage trolley	**bagasiekarretjie**	[baχasi karreki]
passport	**paspoort**	[paspoərt]
visa	**visum**	[fisum]
ticket	**kaartjie**	[kãrki]
air ticket	**lugkaartjie**	[luχ·kãrki]
guidebook	**reisgids**	[ræjsχids]
map (tourist ~)	**kaart**	[kãrt]
area (rural ~)	**gebied**	[χebit]
place, site	**plek**	[plek]
exotica (n)	**eksotiese dinge**	[ɛksotisə diŋə]
exotic (adj)	**eksoties**	[ɛksotis]
amazing (adj)	**verbasend**	[ferbasent]
group	**groep**	[χrup]
excursion, sightseeing tour	**uitstappie**	[œitstappi]
guide (person)	**gids**	[χids]

21. Hotel

hotel	**hotel**	[hotəl]
motel	**motel**	[motəl]
three-star (~ hotel)	**drie-ster**	[dri-stər]

| five-star | vyf-ster | [fajf-stər] |
| to stay (in a hotel, etc.) | oornag | [oərnaχ] |

room	kamer	[kamər]
single room	enkelkamer	[ɛnkəl·kamər]
double room	dubbelkamer	[dubbəl·kamər]

| half board | met aandete, bed en ontbyt | [met āndetə], [bet en ontbajt] |
| full board | volle losies | [follə losis] |

with bath	met bad	[met bat]
with shower	met stortbad	[met stort·bat]
satellite television	satelliet-TV	[satɛllit-te·fe]
air-conditioner	lugversorger	[luχfersorχər]
towel	handdoek	[handduk]
key	sleutel	[sløətəl]

administrator	bestuurder	[bestɪrdər]
chambermaid	kamermeisie	[kamər·mæjsi]
porter	hoteljoggie	[hotəl·joχi]
doorman	portier	[portir]

restaurant	restaurant	[restɔurant]
pub, bar	kroeg	[kruχ]
breakfast	ontbyt	[ontbajt]
dinner	aandete	[āndetə]
buffet	buffetete	[buffetetə]

| lobby | voorportaal | [foər·portāl] |
| lift | hysbak | [hajsbak] |

| DO NOT DISTURB | MOENIE STEUR NIE | [muni støər ni] |
| NO SMOKING | ROOK VERBODE | [roək ferbodə] |

22. Sightseeing

monument	monument	[monument]
fortress	fort	[fort]
palace	paleis	[palæjs]
castle	kasteel	[kasteəl]
tower	toring	[toriŋ]
mausoleum	mausoleum	[mɔusoløəm]

architecture	argitektuur	[arχitektɪr]
medieval (adj)	Middeleeus	[middeliʊs]
ancient (adj)	oud	[æʊt]
national (adj)	nasionaal	[naʃionāl]
famous (monument, etc.)	bekend	[bekent]

tourist	toeris	[turis]
guide (person)	gids	[χids]
excursion, sightseeing tour	uitstappie	[œitstappi]
to show (vt)	wys	[vajs]
to tell (vt)	vertel	[fertəl]

to find (vt)	vind	[fint]
to get lost (lose one's way)	verdwaal	[ferdwāl]
map (e.g. underground ~)	kaart	[kārt]
map (e.g. city ~)	kaart	[kārt]

souvenir, gift	aandenking	[āndenkiŋ]
gift shop	geskenkwinkel	[χeskɛnk·vinkəl]
to take pictures	fotografeer	[fotoχrafeər]
to have one's picture taken	jou portret laat maak	[jæʊ portret lāt māk]

TRANSPORT

23. Airport

airport	lughawe	[luχhavə]
aeroplane	vliegtuig	[fliχtœiχ]
airline	lugredery	[luχrederaj]
air traffic controller	lugverkeersleier	[luχ·ferkeərs·læjer]
departure	vertrek	[fertrek]
arrival	aankoms	[ānkoms]
to arrive (by plane)	aankom	[ānkom]
departure time	vertrektyd	[fertrək·tajt]
arrival time	aankomstyd	[ānkoms·tajt]
to be delayed	vertraag wees	[fertrāχ veəs]
flight delay	vlugvertraging	[fluχ·fertraχiŋ]
information board	informasiebord	[informasi·bort]
information	informasie	[informasi]
to announce (vt)	aankondig	[ānkondəχ]
flight (e.g. next ~)	vlug	[fluχ]
customs	doeane	[duanə]
customs officer	doeanebeampte	[duanə·beamptə]
customs declaration	doeaneverklaring	[duanə·ferklariŋ]
to fill in (vt)	invul	[inful]
passport control	paspoortkontrole	[paspoərt·kontrolə]
luggage	bagasie	[baχasi]
hand luggage	handbagasie	[hand·baχasi]
luggage trolley	bagasiekarretjie	[baχasi·karrəki]
landing	landing	[landiŋ]
landing strip	landingsbaan	[landiŋs·bān]
to land (vi)	land	[lant]
airstairs	vliegtuigtrap	[fliχtœiχ·trap]
check-in	na die vertrektoonbank	[na di fertrək·toənbank]
check-in counter	vertrektoonbank	[fertrək·toənbank]
to check-in (vi)	na die vertrektoonbank gaan	[na di fertrək·toənbank χān]
boarding card	instapkaart	[instap·kārt]
departure gate	vertrekuitgang	[fertrek·œitχaŋ]
transit	transito	[traŋsito]
to wait (vt)	wag	[vaχ]
departure lounge	vertreksaal	[fertrək·sāl]

| to see off | afsien | [afsin] |
| to say goodbye | afskeid neem | [afskæjt neəm] |

24. Aeroplane

aeroplane	vliegtuig	[fliχtœiχ]
air ticket	lugkaartjie	[luχ·kārki]
airline	lugredery	[luχrederəj]
airport	lughawe	[luχhavə]
supersonic (adj)	supersonies	[supersonis]

captain	kaptein	[kaptæjn]
crew	bemanning	[bemanniŋ]
pilot	piloot	[piloət]
stewardess	lugwaardin	[luχ·wārdin]
navigator	navigator	[nafiχator]

wings	vlerke	[flerkə]
tail	stert	[stert]
cockpit	stuurkajuit	[stɪr·kajœit]
engine	enjin	[ɛndʒin]
undercarriage (landing gear)	landingstel	[landiŋ·stəl]
turbine	turbine	[turbinə]
propeller	skroef	[skruf]
black box	swart boks	[swart boks]
yoke (control column)	stuurstang	[stɪr·staŋ]
fuel	brandstof	[brantstof]

safety card	veiligheidskaart	[fæjliχæjts·kārt]
oxygen mask	suurstofmasker	[sɪrstof·maskər]
uniform	uniform	[uniform]
lifejacket	reddingsbaadjie	[rɛddiŋs·bādʒi]
parachute	valskerm	[fal·skerm]
takeoff	opstyging	[opstajχiŋ]
to take off (vi)	opstyg	[opstajχ]
runway	landingsbaan	[landiŋs·bān]

visibility	uitsig	[œitsəχ]
flight (act of flying)	vlug	[fluχ]
altitude	hoogte	[hoəχtə]
air pocket	lugsak	[luχsak]

seat	sitplek	[sitplek]
headphones	koptelefoon	[kop·telefoən]
folding tray (tray table)	voutafeltjie	[fæʊ·tafɛlki]
airplane window	vliegtuigvenster	[fliχtœiχ·fɛŋstər]
aisle	paadjie	[pãdʒi]

25. Train

| train | trein | [træjn] |
| commuter train | voorstedelike trein | [foərstedelikə træjn] |

express train	**sneltrein**	[snɛl·træjn]
diesel locomotive	**diesellokomotief**	[disəl·lokomotif]
steam locomotive	**stoomlokomotief**	[stoəm·lokomotif]
coach, carriage	**passasierswa**	[passasirs·wa]
buffet car	**eetwa**	[eet·wa]
rails	**spoorstawe**	[spoər·stavə]
railway	**spoorweg**	[spoər·weχ]
sleeper (track support)	**dwarslêer**	[dwarslɛər]
platform (railway ~)	**perron**	[perron]
platform (~ 1, 2, etc.)	**spoor**	[spoər]
semaphore	**semafoor**	[semafoər]
station	**stasie**	[stasi]
train driver	**treindrywer**	[træjn·drajvər]
porter (of luggage)	**portier**	[portir]
carriage attendant	**kondukteur**	[konduktøər]
passenger	**passasier**	[passasir]
ticket inspector	**kondukteur**	[konduktøər]
corridor (in train)	**gang**	[χaŋ]
emergency brake	**noodrem**	[noədrem]
compartment	**kompartiment**	[kompartiment]
berth	**bed**	[bet]
upper berth	**boonste bed**	[boəŋstə bet]
lower berth	**onderste bed**	[ondərstə bet]
bed linen, bedding	**beddegoed**	[beddə·χut]
ticket	**kaartjie**	[kārki]
timetable	**diensrooster**	[diŋs·roəstər]
information display	**informasiebord**	[informasi·bort]
to leave, to depart	**vertrek**	[fertrek]
departure (of train)	**vertrek**	[fertrek]
to arrive (ab. train)	**aankom**	[ānkom]
arrival	**aankoms**	[ānkoms]
to arrive by train	**aankom per trein**	[ānkom pər træjn]
to get on the train	**in die trein klim**	[in di træjn klim]
to get off the train	**uit die trein klim**	[œit di træjn klim]
train crash	**treinbotsing**	[træjn·botsiŋ]
to derail (vi)	**ontspoor**	[ontspoər]
steam locomotive	**stoomlokomotief**	[stoəm·lokomotif]
stoker, fireman	**stoker**	[stokər]
firebox	**stookplek**	[stoəkplek]
coal	**steenkool**	[steən·koəl]

26. Ship

ship	**skip**	[skip]
vessel	**vaartuig**	[fārtœiχ]

steamship	**stoomboot**	[stoəm·boət]
riverboat	**rivierboot**	[rifir·boət]
cruise ship	**toerskip**	[tur·skip]
cruiser	**kruiser**	[krœisər]
yacht	**jag**	[jaχ]
tugboat	**sleepboot**	[sleəp·boət]
barge	**vragskuit**	[fraχ·skœit]
ferry	**veerboot**	[feər·boət]
sailing ship	**seilskip**	[sæjl·skip]
brigantine	**skoenerbrik**	[skunər·brik]
ice breaker	**ysbreker**	[ajs·brekər]
submarine	**duikboot**	[dœik·boət]
boat (flat-bottomed ~)	**roeiboot**	[ruiboət]
dinghy	**bootjie**	[boəki]
lifeboat	**reddingsboot**	[rɛddiŋs·boət]
motorboat	**motorboot**	[motor·boət]
captain	**kaptein**	[kaptæjn]
seaman	**seeman**	[seəman]
sailor	**matroos**	[matroəs]
crew	**bemanning**	[bemanniŋ]
boatswain	**bootsman**	[boətsman]
ship's boy	**skeepsjonge**	[skeəps·joŋə]
cook	**kok**	[kok]
ship's doctor	**skeepsdokter**	[skoopc·doktər]
deck	**dek**	[dek]
mast	**mas**	[mas]
sail	**seil**	[sæjl]
hold	**skeepsruim**	[skeəps·rœim]
bow (prow)	**boeg**	[buχ]
stern	**agterstewe**	[aχtərstevə]
oar	**roeispaan**	[ruis·pān]
screw propeller	**skroef**	[skruf]
cabin	**kajuit**	[kajœit]
wardroom	**offisierskajuit**	[offisirs·kajœit]
engine room	**enjinkamer**	[ɛndʒin·kamər]
bridge	**brug**	[bruχ]
radio room	**radiokamer**	[radio·kamər]
wave (radio)	**golf**	[χolf]
logbook	**logboek**	[loχbuk]
spyglass	**verkyker**	[ferkajkər]
bell	**bel**	[bəl]
flag	**vlag**	[flaχ]
hawser (mooring ~)	**kabel**	[kabəl]
knot (bowline, etc.)	**knoop**	[knoəp]
deckrails	**dekleuning**	[dek·løəniŋ]

gangway	**gangplank**	[χaŋ·plank]
anchor	**anker**	[ankər]
to weigh anchor	**anker lig**	[ankər ləχ]
to drop anchor	**anker uitgooi**	[ankər œitχoj]
anchor chain	**ankerketting**	[ankər·kɛttiŋ]
port (harbour)	**hawe**	[havə]
quay, wharf	**kaai**	[kãi]
to berth (moor)	**vasmeer**	[fasmeər]
to cast off	**vertrek**	[fertrek]
trip, voyage	**reis**	[ræjs]
cruise (sea trip)	**cruise**	[kru:s]
course (route)	**koers**	[kurs]
route (itinerary)	**roete**	[rutə]
fairway (safe water channel)	**vaarwater**	[fãr·vatər]
shallows	**sandbank**	[sand·bank]
to run aground	**strand**	[strant]
storm	**storm**	[storm]
signal	**sienjaal**	[sinjãl]
to sink (vi)	**sink**	[sink]
Man overboard!	**Man oorboord!**	[man oərboərd!]
SOS (distress signal)	**SOS**	[sos]
ring buoy	**reddingsboei**	[rɛddiŋs·bui]

CITY

27. Urban transport

bus, coach	**bus**	[bus]
tram	**trem**	[trem]
trolleybus	**trembus**	[trembus]
route (of bus, etc.)	**busroete**	[bus·rutə]
number (e.g. bus ~)	**nommer**	[nommər]
to go by ...	**ry per ...**	[raj pər ...]
to get on (~ the bus)	**inklim**	[inklim]
to get off ...	**uitklim ...**	[œitklim ...]
stop (e.g. bus ~)	**halte**	[haltə]
next stop	**volgende halte**	[folχendə haltə]
terminus	**eindpunt**	[æjnd·punt]
timetable	**diensrooster**	[diŋs·roəstər]
to wait (vt)	**wag**	[vaχ]
ticket	**kaartjie**	[kārki]
fare	**reistarief**	[ræjs·tarif]
cashier (ticket seller)	**kaartjleverkoper**	[kārki·forkopor]
ticket inspection	**kaartjiekontrole**	[kārki·kontrolə]
ticket inspector	**kontroleur**	[kontroløər]
to be late (for ...)	**laat wees**	[lāt veəs]
to miss (~ the train, etc.)	**mis**	[mis]
to be in a hurry	**haastig wees**	[hāstəχ veəs]
taxi, cab	**taxi**	[taksi]
taxi driver	**taxibestuurder**	[taksi·bestɪrdər]
by taxi	**per taxi**	[pər taksi]
taxi rank	**taxistaanplek**	[taksi·stānplek]
traffic	**verkeer**	[ferkeər]
traffic jam	**verkeersknoop**	[ferkeərs·knoəp]
rush hour	**spitsuur**	[spits·ɪr]
to park (vi)	**parkeer**	[parkeər]
to park (vt)	**parkeer**	[parkeər]
car park	**parkeerterrein**	[parkeər·terræjn]
underground, tube	**metro**	[metro]
station	**stasie**	[stasi]
to take the tube	**die metro vat**	[di metro fat]
train	**trein**	[træjn]
train station	**treinstasie**	[træjn·stasi]

28. City. Life in the city

city, town	**stad**	[stat]
capital city	**hoofstad**	[hoəf·stat]
village	**dorp**	[dorp]
city map	**stadskaart**	[stats·kãrt]
city centre	**sentrum**	[sentrum]
suburb	**voorstad**	[foərstat]
suburban (adj)	**voorstedelik**	[foərstedelik]
outskirts	**buitewyke**	[bœitəvajkə]
environs (suburbs)	**omgewing**	[omχeviŋ]
city block	**stadswyk**	[stats·wajk]
residential block (area)	**woonbuurt**	[voənbɪrt]
traffic	**verkeer**	[ferkeər]
traffic lights	**robot**	[robot]
public transport	**openbare vervoer**	[openbarə ferfur]
crossroads	**kruispunt**	[krœis·punt]
zebra crossing	**sebraoorgang**	[sebra·oərχaŋ]
pedestrian subway	**voetgangertonnel**	[futχaŋər·tonnəl]
to cross (~ the street)	**oorsteek**	[oərsteək]
pedestrian	**voetganger**	[futχaŋər]
pavement	**sypaadjie**	[saj·pãdʒi]
bridge	**brug**	[bruχ]
embankment (river walk)	**wal**	[val]
fountain	**fontein**	[fontæjn]
allée (garden walkway)	**laning**	[laniŋ]
park	**park**	[park]
boulevard	**boulevard**	[bulefar]
square	**plein**	[plæjn]
avenue (wide street)	**laan**	[lãn]
street	**straat**	[strãt]
side street	**systraat**	[saj·strãt]
dead end	**doodloopstraat**	[doədloəp·strãt]
house	**huis**	[hœis]
building	**gebou**	[χebæʊ]
skyscraper	**wolkekrabber**	[volkə·krabbər]
facade	**gewel**	[χevəl]
roof	**dak**	[dak]
window	**venster**	[fɛŋstər]
arch	**arkade**	[arkadə]
column	**kolom**	[kolom]
corner	**hoek**	[huk]
shop window	**uitstalraam**	[œitstalrãm]
signboard (store sign, etc.)	**reklamebord**	[reklamə·bort]
poster	**plakkaat**	[plakkãt]
advertising poster	**reklameplakkaat**	[reklamə·plakkãt]

hoarding	**aanplakbord**	[ānplakbort]
rubbish	**vullis**	[fullis]
rubbish bin	**vullisbak**	[fullis·bak]
to litter (vi)	**rommel strooi**	[rommel stroj]
rubbish dump	**vullishoop**	[fullis·hoəp]
telephone box	**telefoonhokkie**	[telefoən·hokki]
lamppost	**lamppaal**	[lamp·pāl]
bench (park ~)	**bank**	[bank]
police officer	**polisieman**	[polisi·man]
police	**polisie**	[polisi]
beggar	**bedelaar**	[bedelār]
homeless (n)	**daklose**	[daklosə]

29. Urban institutions

shop	**winkel**	[vinkəl]
chemist, pharmacy	**apteek**	[apteək]
optician (spectacles shop)	**optisiên**	[optisiɛn]
shopping centre	**winkelsentrum**	[vinkəl·sentrum]
supermarket	**supermark**	[supermark]
bakery	**bakkery**	[bakkeraj]
baker	**bakker**	[bakkər]
cake shop	**banketbakkery**	[banket·bakkeraj]
grocery shop	**kruidenierswinkel**	[krœidenirs·vinkəl]
butcher shop	**slagter**	[slaχtor]
greengrocer	**groentewinkel**	[χruntə·vinkəl]
market	**mark**	[mark]
coffee bar	**koffiekroeg**	[koffi·kruχ]
restaurant	**restaurant**	[restɔurant]
pub, bar	**kroeg**	[kruχ]
pizzeria	**pizzeria**	[pizzeria]
hairdresser	**haarsalon**	[hār·salon]
post office	**poskantoor**	[pos·kantoər]
dry cleaners	**droogskoonmakers**	[droəχ·skoən·makers]
photo studio	**fotostudio**	[foto·studio]
shoe shop	**skoenwinkel**	[skun·vinkəl]
bookshop	**boekhandel**	[buk·handəl]
sports shop	**sportwinkel**	[sport·vinkəl]
clothes repair shop	**klereherstelwinkel**	[klerə·herstəl·vinkəl]
formal wear hire	**klereverhuurwinkel**	[klerə·ferhɪr·vinkəl]
video rental shop	**videowinkel**	[video·vinkəl]
circus	**sirkus**	[sirkus]
zoo	**dieretuin**	[dirə·tœin]
cinema	**bioskoop**	[bioskoəp]
museum	**museum**	[musøəm]

library	biblioteek	[biblioteək]
theatre	teater	[teatər]
opera (opera house)	opera	[opera]
nightclub	nagklub	[naχ·klup]
casino	kasino	[kasino]

mosque	moskee	[moskeə]
synagogue	sinagoge	[sinaχoχə]
cathedral	katedraal	[katedrāl]
temple	tempel	[tempəl]
church	kerk	[kerk]

college	kollege	[kolledʒ]
university	universiteit	[unifersitæjt]
school	skool	[skoəl]

prefecture	stadhuis	[stat·hœis]
town hall	stadhuis	[stat·hœis]
hotel	hotel	[hotəl]
bank	bank	[bank]

embassy	ambassade	[ambassadə]
travel agency	reisagentskap	[ræjs·aχentskap]
information office	inligtingskantoor	[inliχtiŋs·kantoər]
currency exchange	wisselkantoor	[vissəl·kantoər]

| underground, tube | metro | [metro] |
| hospital | hospitaal | [hospitāl] |

| petrol station | petrolstasie | [petrol·stasi] |
| car park | parkeerterrein | [parkeər·terræjn] |

30. Signs

signboard (store sign, etc.)	reklamebord	[reklamə·bort]
notice (door sign, etc.)	kennisgewing	[kɛnnis·χeviŋ]
poster	plakkaat	[plakkāt]
direction sign	rigtingwyser	[riχtiŋ·wajsər]
arrow (sign)	pyl	[pajl]

caution	waarskuwing	[vārskuviŋ]
warning sign	waarskuwingsbord	[vārskuviŋs·bort]
to warn (vt)	waarsku	[vārsku]

rest day (weekly ~)	rusdag	[rusdaχ]
timetable (schedule)	diensrooster	[diŋs·roəstər]
opening hours	besigheidsure	[besiχæjts·urə]

WELCOME!	WELKOM!	[vɛlkom!]
ENTRANCE	INGANG	[inχaŋ]
WAY OUT	UITGANG	[œitχaŋ]

| PUSH | STOOT | [stoət] |
| PULL | TREK | [trek] |

| OPEN | OOP | [oəp] |
| CLOSED | GESLUIT | [χeslœit] |

| WOMEN | DAMES | [dames] |
| MEN | MANS | [maŋs] |

DISCOUNTS	AFSLAG	[afslaχ]
SALE	UITVERKOPING	[œitferkopiŋ]
NEW!	NUUT!	[nɪt!]
FREE	GRATIS	[χratis]

ATTENTION!	PAS OP!	[pas op!]
NO VACANCIES	VOLBESPREEK	[folbespreək]
RESERVED	BESPREEK	[bespreək]

| ADMINISTRATION | ADMINISTRASIE | [administrasi] |
| STAFF ONLY | SLEGS PERSONEEL | [sleχs personeəl] |

BEWARE OF THE DOG!	PAS OP VIR DIE HOND!	[pas op fir di hont!]
NO SMOKING	ROOK VERBODE	[roək ferbodə]
DO NOT TOUCH!	NIE AANRAAK NIE!	[ni ānrāk ni!]

DANGEROUS	GEVAARLIK	[χefārlik]
DANGER	GEVAAR	[χefār]
HIGH VOLTAGE	HOOGSPANNING	[hoəχ·spanniŋ]
NO SWIMMING!	NIE SWEM NIE	[ni swem ni]
OUT OF ORDER	BUITE WERKING	[bœitə verkiŋ]

FLAMMABLE	ONTVLAMBAAR	[ontflambār]
FORBIDDEN	VERBODE	[ferbodə]
NO TRESPASSING!	TOEGANG VERBODE!	[tuχaŋ ferbode!]
WET PAINT	NAT VERF	[nat ferf]

31. Shopping

to buy (purchase)	koop	[koəp]
shopping	aankoop	[ānkoəp]
to go shopping	inkopies doen	[inkopis dun]
shopping	inkoop	[inkoəp]

| to be open (ab. shop) | oop wees | [oəp veəs] |
| to be closed | toe wees | [tu veəs] |

footwear, shoes	skoeisel	[skuisəl]
clothes, clothing	klere	[klerə]
cosmetics	kosmetika	[kosmetika]
food products	voedingsware	[fudiŋs·warə]
gift, present	present	[present]

| shop assistant (masc.) | verkoper | [ferkopər] |
| shop assistant (fem.) | verkoopsdame | [ferkoəps·damə] |

| cash desk | kassier | [kassir] |
| mirror | spieël | [spicl] |

| counter (shop ~) | toonbank | [toən·bank] |
| fitting room | paskamer | [pas·kamər] |

to try on	aanpas	[ānpas]
to fit (ab. dress, etc.)	pas	[pas]
to fancy (vt)	hou van	[hæʊ fan]

price	prys	[prajs]
price tag	pryskaartjie	[prajs·kārki]
to cost (vt)	kos	[kos]
How much?	Hoeveel?	[hufeəl?]
discount	afslag	[afslaχ]

inexpensive (adj)	billik	[billik]
cheap (adj)	goedkoop	[χudkoəp]
expensive (adj)	duur	[dɪr]
It's expensive	dis duur	[dis dɪr]

hire (n)	verhuur	[ferhɪr]
to hire (~ a dinner jacket)	verhuur	[ferhɪr]
credit (trade credit)	krediet	[krediet]
on credit (adv)	op krediet	[op krediet]

CLOTHING & ACCESSORIES

32. Outerwear. Coats

clothes	klere	[klerə]
outerwear	oorklere	[oərklerə]
winter clothing	winterklere	[vintər·klerə]
coat (overcoat)	jas	[jas]
fur coat	pelsjas	[pelʃas]
fur jacket	kort pelsjas	[kort pelʃas]
down coat	donsjas	[donʃas]
jacket (e.g. leather ~)	baadjie	[bādʒi]
raincoat (trenchcoat, etc.)	reënjas	[rɛnjas]
waterproof (adj)	waterdig	[vatərdəχ]

33. Men's & women's clothing

shirt (button shirt)	hemp	[hemp]
trousers	broek	[bruk]
jeans	denimbroek	[denim bruk]
suit jacket	baadjie	[bādʒi]
suit	pak	[pak]
dress (frock)	rok	[rok]
skirt	romp	[romp]
blouse	bloes	[blus]
knitted jacket (cardigan, etc.)	gebreide baadjie	[χebræjdə bādʒi]
jacket (of woman's suit)	baadjie	[bādʒi]
T-shirt	T-hemp	[te-hemp]
shorts (short trousers)	kortbroek	[kort·bruk]
tracksuit	sweetpak	[sweət·pak]
bathrobe	badjas	[batjas]
pyjamas	pajama	[pajama]
jumper (sweater)	trui	[trœi]
pullover	trui	[trœi]
waistcoat	onderbaadjie	[ondər·bādʒi]
tailcoat	swaelstertbaadjie	[swaɛlstert·bādʒi]
dinner suit	aandpak	[āntpak]
uniform	uniform	[uniform]
workwear	werksklere	[verks·klerə]
boiler suit	oorpak	[oərpak]
coat (e.g. doctor's smock)	jas	[jas]

34. Clothing. Underwear

underwear	onderklere	[ondərklerə]
pants	onderbroek	[ondərbruk]
panties	onderbroek	[ondərbruk]
vest (singlet)	frokkie	[frokki]
socks	sokkies	[sokkis]
nightgown	nagrok	[naχrok]
bra	bra	[bra]
knee highs (knee-high socks)	kniekouse	[kni·kæʊsə]
tights	kousbroek	[kæʊsbruk]
stockings (hold ups)	kouse	[kæʊsə]
swimsuit, bikini	baaikostuum	[bāj·kostɪm]

35. Headwear

hat	hoed	[hut]
trilby hat	hoed	[hut]
baseball cap	bofbalpet	[bofbal·pet]
flatcap	pet	[pet]
beret	mus	[mus]
hood	kap	[kap]
panama hat	panamahoed	[panama·hut]
knit cap (knitted hat)	gebreide mus	[χebræjdə mus]
headscarf	kopdoek	[kopduk]
women's hat	dameshoed	[dames·hut]
hard hat	veiligheidshelm	[fæjliχæjts·hɛlm]
forage cap	mus	[mus]
helmet	helmet	[hɛlmet]
bowler	bolhoed	[bolhut]
top hat	hoëhoed	[hoɛhut]

36. Footwear

footwear	skoeisel	[skuisəl]
shoes (men's shoes)	mansskoene	[maŋs·skunə]
shoes (women's shoes)	damesskoene	[dames·skunə]
boots (e.g., cowboy ~)	laarse	[lārsə]
carpet slippers	pantoffels	[pantoffəls]
trainers	tennisskoene	[tɛnnis·skunə]
trainers	tekkies	[tɛkkis]
sandals	sandale	[sandalə]
cobbler (shoe repairer)	skoenmaker	[skun·makər]
heel	hak	[hak]

pair (of shoes)	paar	[pãr]
lace (shoelace)	skoenveter	[skun·fetər]
to lace up (vt)	ryg	[rajχ]
shoehorn	skoenlepel	[skun·lepəl]
shoe polish	skoenpolitoer	[skun·politur]

37. Personal accessories

gloves	handskoene	[ɦandskunə]
mittens	duimhandskoene	[dœim·ɦandskunə]
scarf (muffler)	serp	[serp]

glasses	bril	[bril]
frame (eyeglass ~)	raam	[rãm]
umbrella	sambreel	[sambreəl]
walking stick	wandelstok	[vandəl·stok]
hairbrush	haarborsel	[hãr·borsəl]
fan	waaier	[vãjer]

tie (necktie)	das	[das]
bow tie	strikkie	[strikki]
braces	kruisbande	[krœis·bandə]
handkerchief	sakdoek	[sakduk]

comb	kam	[kam]
hair slide	haarspeld	[hãrs·pɛlt]
hairpin	haarpen	[hãr·pen]
buckle	gespe	[χespə]

| belt | belt | [bɛlt] |
| shoulder strap | skouerband | [skæuer·bant] |

bag (handbag)	handsak	[hand·sak]
handbag	beursie	[bøərsi]
rucksack	rugsak	[ruχsak]

38. Clothing. Miscellaneous

fashion	mode	[modə]
in vogue (adj)	in die mode	[in di modə]
fashion designer	modeontwerper	[mode·ontwerpər]

collar	kraag	[krãχ]
pocket	sak	[sak]
pocket (as adj)	sak-	[sak-]
sleeve	mou	[mæu]
hanging loop	lussie	[lussi]
flies (on trousers)	gulp	[χulp]

zip (fastener)	ritssluiter	[rits·slœitər]
fastener	vasmaker	[fasmakər]
button	knoop	[knoəp]

| buttonhole | knoopsgat | [knoəps·χat] |
| to come off (ab. button) | loskom | [loskom] |

to sew (vi, vt)	naai	[nãi]
to embroider (vi, vt)	borduur	[bordɪr]
embroidery	borduurwerk	[bordɪr·werk]
sewing needle	naald	[nãlt]
thread	garing	[χariŋ]
seam	soom	[soəm]

to get dirty (vi)	vuil word	[fœil vort]
stain (mark, spot)	vlek	[flek]
to crease, crumple (vi)	kreukel	[krøəkəl]
to tear, to rip (vt)	skeur	[skøər]
clothes moth	mot	[mot]

39. Personal care. Cosmetics

toothpaste	tandepasta	[tandə·pasta]
toothbrush	tandeborsel	[tandə·borsəl]
to clean one's teeth	tande borsel	[tandə borsəl]

razor	skeermes	[skeər·mes]
shaving cream	skeerroom	[skeər·roəm]
to shave (vi)	skeer	[skeər]

| soap | seep | [seəp] |
| shampoo | sjampoe | [ʃampu] |

scissors	skèr	[skær]
nail file	naelvyl	[naɛl·fajl]
nail clippers	naelknipper	[naɛl·knippər]
tweezers	haartangetjie	[hãrtaŋəki]

cosmetics	kosmetika	[kosmetika]
face mask	gesigmasker	[χesiχ·maskər]
manicure	manikuur	[manikɪr]
to have a manicure	laat manikuur	[lãt manikɪr]
pedicure	voetbehandeling	[fut·behandeliŋ]

make-up bag	kosmetika tassie	[kosmetika tassi]
face powder	gesigpoeier	[χesiχ·pujer]
powder compact	poeierdosie	[pujer·dosi]
blusher	blosser	[blossər]

perfume (bottled)	parfuum	[parfɪm]
toilet water (lotion)	reukwater	[røək·vatər]
lotion	vloeiroom	[flui·roəm]
cologne	reukwater	[røək·vatər]

eyeshadow	oogskadu	[oəχ·skadu]
eyeliner	oogomlyner	[oəχ·omlajnər]
mascara	maskara	[maskara]
lipstick	lipstiffie	[lip·stiffi]

nail polish	**naellak**	[naɛl·lak]
hair spray	**haarsproei**	[hārs·prui]
deodorant	**reukweermiddel**	[røək·veərmiddəl]
cream	**room**	[roəm]
face cream	**gesigroom**	[χesiχ·roəm]
hand cream	**handroom**	[hand·roəm]
anti-wrinkle cream	**antirimpelroom**	[antirimpəl·roəm]
day cream	**dagroom**	[daχ·roəm]
night cream	**nagroom**	[naχ·roəm]
day (as adj)	**dag-**	[daχ-]
night (as adj)	**nag-**	[naχ-]
tampon	**tampon**	[tampon]
toilet paper (toilet roll)	**toiletpapier**	[tojlet·papir]
hair dryer	**haardroër**	[hār·droɛr]

40. Watches. Clocks

watch (wristwatch)	**polshorlosie**	[pols·horlosi]
dial	**wyserplaat**	[vajsər·plāt]
hand (of clock, watch)	**wyster**	[vajstər]
metal bracelet	**metaal horlosiebandjie**	[metāl horlosi·bandʒi]
watch strap	**horlosiebandjie**	[horlosi·bandʒi]
battery	**battery**	[battəraj]
to be flat (battery)	**pap wees**	[pap veəs]
to run fast	**voorloop**	[foərloʉp]
to run slow	**agterloop**	[aχtərloəp]
wall clock	**muurhorlosie**	[mɪr·horlosi]
hourglass	**uurglas**	[ɪr·χlas]
sundial	**sonwyser**	[son·wajsər]
alarm clock	**wekker**	[vɛkkər]
watchmaker	**horlosiemaker**	[horlosi·makər]
to repair (vt)	**herstel**	[herstəl]

EVERYDAY EXPERIENCE

41. Money

money	geld	[χɛlt]
currency exchange	valutaruil	[faluta·rœil]
exchange rate	wisselkoers	[vissəl·kurs]
cashpoint	OTM	[o·te·em]
coin	muntstuk	[muntstuk]
dollar	dollar	[dollar]
euro	euro	[øəro]
lira	lira	[lira]
Deutschmark	Duitse mark	[dœitsə mark]
franc	frank	[frank]
pound sterling	pond sterling	[pont sterliŋ]
yen	yen	[jɛn]
debt	skuld	[skult]
debtor	skuldenaar	[skuldenãr]
to lend (money)	uitleen	[œitleən]
to borrow (vi, vt)	leen	[leən]
bank	bank	[bank]
account	rekening	[rekəniŋ]
to deposit (vt)	deponeer	[deponeər]
to withdraw (vt)	trek	[trek]
credit card	kredietkaart	[kredit·kãrt]
cash	kontant	[kontant]
cheque	tjek	[ʧek]
chequebook	tjekboek	[ʧek·buk]
wallet	beursie	[bøərsi]
purse	muntstukbeursie	[muntstuk·bøərsi]
safe	brandkas	[brant·kas]
heir	erfgenaam	[ɛrfχənãm]
inheritance	erfenis	[ɛrfenis]
fortune (wealth)	fortuin	[fortœin]
lease	huur	[hɪr]
rent (money)	huur	[hɪr]
to rent (sth from sb)	huur	[hɪr]
price	prys	[prajs]
cost	prys	[prajs]
sum	som	[som]
to spend (vt)	spandeer	[spandeər]

expenses	onkoste	[onkostə]
to economize (vi, vt)	besuinig	[besœinəχ]
economical	ekonomies	[ɛkonomis]

to pay (vi, vt)	betaal	[betãl]
payment	betaling	[betaliŋ]
change (give the ~)	wisselgeld	[vissəl·χɛlt]

tax	belasting	[belastiŋ]
fine	boete	[butə]
to fine (vt)	beboet	[bebut]

42. Post. Postal service

post office	poskantoor	[pos·kantoər]
post (letters, etc.)	pos	[pos]
postman	posbode	[pos·bodə]
opening hours	besigheidsure	[besiχæjts·urə]

letter	brief	[brif]
registered letter	geregistreerde brief	[χereχistreərdə brif]
postcard	poskaart	[pos·kãrt]
telegram	telegram	[teleχram]
parcel	pakkie	[pakki]
money transfer	geldoorplasing	[χɛld·oərplasiŋ]

to receive (vt)	ontvang	[ontfaŋ]
to send (vt)	stuur	[stɪr]
sending	versending	[fersendiŋ]

address	adres	[adres]
postcode	poskode	[pos·kodə]
sender	sender	[sendər]
receiver	ontvanger	[ontfaŋər]

| name (first name) | voornaam | [foərnãm] |
| surname (last name) | van | [fan] |

postage rate	postarief	[pos·tarif]
standard (adj)	standaard	[standãrt]
economical (adj)	ekonomies	[ɛkonomis]

weight	gewig	[χevəχ]
to weigh (~ letters)	weeg	[veeχ]
envelope	koevert	[kufert]
postage stamp	posseël	[pos·seɛl]

43. Banking

bank	bank	[bank]
branch (of bank, etc.)	tak	[tak]
consultant	bankklerk	[bank·klerk]

manager (director)	bestuurder	[bestɪrdər]
bank account	bankrekening	[bank·rekəniŋ]
account number	rekeningnommer	[rekəniŋ·nommər]
current account	tjekrekening	[ʧek·rekəniŋ]
deposit account	spaarrekening	[spãr·rekəniŋ]

| to close the account | die rekening sluit | [di rekəniŋ slœit] |
| to withdraw (vt) | trek | [trek] |

deposit	deposito	[deposito]
wire transfer	telegrafiese oorplasing	[teleχrafisə oərplasiŋ]
to wire, to transfer	oorplaas	[oərplãs]

| sum | som | [som] |
| How much? | Hoeveel? | [hufeəl?] |

| signature | handtekening | [hand·tekəniŋ] |
| to sign (vt) | onderteken | [ondərtekən] |

credit card	kredietkaart	[kredit·kãrt]
code (PIN code)	kode	[kodə]
credit card number	kredietkaartnommer	[kredit·kãrt·nommər]
cashpoint	OTM	[o·te·em]

| cheque | tjek | [ʧek] |
| chequebook | tjekboek | [ʧek·buk] |

| loan (bank ~) | lening | [leniŋ] |
| guarantee | waarborg | [vãrborχ] |

44. Telephone. Phone conversation

telephone	telefoon	[telefoən]
mobile phone	selfoon	[sɛlfoən]
answerphone	antwoordmasjien	[antwoərt·maʃin]

| to call (by phone) | bel | [bəl] |
| call, ring | oproep | [oprup] |

Hello!	Hallo!	[hallo!]
to ask (vt)	vra	[fra]
to answer (vi, vt)	antwoord	[antwoərt]

to hear (vt)	hoor	[hoər]
well (adv)	goed	[χut]
not well (adv)	nie goed nie	[ni χut ni]
noises (interference)	steurings	[støəriŋs]

receiver	gehoorstuk	[χehoərstuk]
to pick up (~ the phone)	optel	[optəl]
to hang up (~ the phone)	afskakel	[afskakəl]

| busy (engaged) | besig | [besəχ] |
| to ring (ab. phone) | lui | [lœi] |

telephone book	telefoongids	[telefoən·χids]
local (adj)	lokale	[lokalə]
local call	lokale oproep	[lokalə oprup]
trunk (e.g. ~ call)	langafstand	[lanχ·afstant]
trunk call	langafstand oproep	[lanχ·afstant oprup]
international (adj)	internasionale	[internaʃionalə]
international call	internasionale oproep	[internaʃionalə oprup]

45. Mobile telephone

mobile phone	selfoon	[sɛlfoən]
display	skerm	[skerm]
button	knoppie	[knoppi]
SIM card	SIMkaart	[sim·kãrt]
battery	battery	[battəraj]
to be flat (battery)	pap wees	[pap veəs]
charger	batterylaaier	[battəraj·lajer]
menu	spyskaart	[spajs·kãrt]
settings	instellings	[instɛlliŋs]
tune (melody)	wysie	[vajsi]
to select (vt)	kies	[kis]
calculator	sakrekenaar	[sakrekənãr]
voice mail	stempos	[stem·pos]
alarm clock	wekker	[vɛkkər]
contacts	kontakte	[kontɑktə]
SMS (text message)	SMS	[es·em·es]
subscriber	intekenaar	[intekənãr]

46. Stationery

ballpoint pen	bolpen	[bol·pen]
fountain pen	vulpen	[ful·pen]
pencil	potlood	[potloət]
highlighter	merkpen	[merk·pen]
felt-tip pen	viltpen	[filt·pen]
notepad	notaboekie	[nota·buki]
diary	dagboek	[daχ·buk]
ruler	liniaal	[liniãl]
calculator	sakrekenaar	[sakrekənãr]
rubber	uitveêr	[œitfeɛr]
drawing pin	duimspyker	[dœim·spajkər]
paper clip	skuifspeld	[skœif·spɛlt]
glue	gom	[χom]
stapler	krammasjien	[kram·maʃin]

| hole punch | ponsmasjien | [poŋs·maʃin] |
| pencil sharpener | skerpmaker | [skerp·makər] |

47. Foreign languages

language	taal	[tãl]
foreign (adj)	vreemd	[freəmt]
foreign language	vreemde taal	[freəmdə tãl]
to study (vt)	studeer	[studeər]
to learn (language, etc.)	leer	[leər]

to read (vi, vt)	lees	[leəs]
to speak (vi, vt)	praat	[prãt]
to understand (vt)	verstaan	[ferstãn]
to write (vt)	skryf	[skrajf]

fast (adv)	vinnig	[finnəx]
slowly (adv)	stadig	[stadəx]
fluently (adv)	vlot	[flot]

rules	reëls	[reɛls]
grammar	grammatika	[xrammatika]
vocabulary	woordeskat	[voərdeskat]
phonetics	fonetika	[fonetika]

textbook	handboek	[hand·buk]
dictionary	woordeboek	[voərdə·buk]
teach-yourself book	selfstudie boek	[sɛlfstudi buk]
phrasebook	taalgids	[tãl·xids]

cassette, tape	kasset	[kasset]
videotape	videoband	[video·bant]
CD, compact disc	CD	[se·de]
DVD	DVD	[de·fe·de]

alphabet	alfabet	[alfabet]
to spell (vt)	spel	[spel]
pronunciation	uitspraak	[œitsprãk]
accent	aksent	[aksent]

| word | woord | [voərt] |
| meaning | betekenis | [betekənis] |

course (e.g. a French ~)	kursus	[kursus]
to sign up	inskryf	[inskrajf]
teacher	onderwyser	[onderwajsər]

translation (process)	vertaling	[fertaliŋ]
translation (text, etc.)	vertaling	[fertaliŋ]
translator	vertaler	[fertalər]
interpreter	tolk	[tolk]

| polyglot | poliglot | [polixlot] |
| memory | geheue | [xəhøə] |

MEALS. RESTAURANT

48. Table setting

spoon	lepel	[lepəl]
knife	mes	[mes]
fork	vurk	[furk]
cup (e.g., coffee ~)	koppie	[koppi]
plate (dinner ~)	bord	[bort]
saucer	piering	[piriŋ]
serviette	servet	[serfət]
toothpick	tandestokkie	[tandə·stokki]

49. Restaurant

restaurant	restaurant	[restɔurant]
coffee bar	koffiekroeg	[koffi·kruχ]
pub, bar	kroeg	[kruχ]
tearoom	teekamer	[teə·kamər]
waiter	kelner	[kɛlnər]
waitress	kelnerin	[kɛlnərin]
barman	kroegman	[kruχman]
menu	spyskaart	[spajs·kārt]
wine list	wyn	[vajn]
to book a table	wynkaart	[vajn·kārt]
course, dish	gereg	[χerəχ]
to order (meal)	bestel	[bestəl]
to make an order	bestel	[bestəl]
aperitif	drankie	[dranki]
starter	voorgereg	[foərχerəχ]
dessert, pudding	nagereg	[naχerəχ]
bill	rekening	[rekəniŋ]
to pay the bill	die rekening betaal	[di rekəniŋ betāl]
to give change	kleingeld gee	[klæjn·χɛlt χeə]
tip	fooitjie	[fojki]

50. Meals

food	kos	[kos]
to eat (vi, vt)	eet	[eət]

breakfast	ontbyt	[ontbajt]
to have breakfast	ontbyt	[ontbajt]
lunch	middagete	[middaχ·etə]
to have lunch	gaan eet	[χān eət]
dinner	aandete	[āndetə]
to have dinner	aandete gebruik	[āndetə χebrœik]

| appetite | aptyt | [aptajt] |
| Enjoy your meal! | Smaaklike ete! | [smāklikə etə!] |

to open (~ a bottle)	oopmaak	[oəpmāk]
to spill (liquid)	mors	[mors]
to spill out (vi)	mors	[mors]

to boil (vi)	kook	[koək]
to boil (vt)	kook	[koək]
boiled (~ water)	gekook	[χekoək]
to chill, cool down (vt)	laat afkoel	[lāt afkul]
to chill (vi)	afkoel	[afkul]

| taste, flavour | smaak | [smāk] |
| aftertaste | nasmaak | [nasmāk] |

to slim down (lose weight)	vermaer	[fermaər]
diet	dieet	[diət]
vitamin	vitamien	[fitamin]
calorie	kalorie	[kalori]
vegetarian (n)	vegetariër	[feχetariɛr]
vegetarian (adj)	vegetaries	[feχetaris]

fats (nutrient)	vette	[fɛttə]
proteins	proteïen	[proteïen]
carbohydrates	koolhidrate	[koəlhidratə]

slice (of lemon, ham)	snytjie	[snajki]
piece (of cake, pie)	stuk	[stuk]
crumb (of bread, cake, etc.)	krummel	[krumməl]

51. Cooked dishes

course, dish	gereg	[χerəχ]
cuisine	kookkuns	[koək·kuns]
recipe	resep	[resep]
portion	porsie	[porsi]

| salad | slaai | [slāi] |
| soup | sop | [sop] |

clear soup (broth)	helder sop	[hɛldər sop]
sandwich (bread)	toebroodjie	[tubroədʒi]
fried eggs	gabakte eiers	[χabaktə æjers]

| hamburger (beefburger) | hamburger | [hamburχər] |
| beefsteak | biefstuk | [bifstuk] |

side dish	sygereg	[saj·χerəχ]
spaghetti	spaghetti	[spaχɛtti]
mash	kapokaartappels	[kapok·ārtappəls]
pizza	pizza	[pizza]
porridge (oatmeal, etc.)	pap	[pap]
omelette	omelet	[oməlet]

boiled (e.g. ~ beef)	gekook	[χekoək]
smoked (adj)	gerook	[χeroək]
fried (adj)	gebak	[χebak]
dried (adj)	gedroog	[χedroəχ]
frozen (adj)	gevries	[χefris]
pickled (adj)	gepiekel	[χepikəl]

sweet (sugary)	soet	[sut]
salty (adj)	sout	[sæʊt]
cold (adj)	koud	[kæʊt]
hot (adj)	warm	[varm]
bitter (adj)	bitter	[bittər]
tasty (adj)	smaaklik	[smāklik]

to cook in boiling water	kook in water	[koək in vatər]
to cook (dinner)	kook	[koək]
to fry (vt)	braai	[braj]
to heat up (food)	opwarm	[opwarm]

to salt (vt)	sout	[sæʊt]
to pepper (vt)	peper	[pepər]
to grate (vt)	rasp	[rasp]
peel (n)	skil	[ɛkil]
to peel (vt)	skil	[skil]

52. Food

meat	vleis	[flæjs]
chicken	hoender	[hundər]
poussin	braaikuiken	[brāj·kœiken]
duck	eend	[eent]
goose	gans	[χaŋs]
game	wild	[vilt]
turkey	kalkoen	[kalkun]

pork	varkvleis	[fark·flæjs]
veal	kalfsvleis	[kalfs·flæjs]
lamb	lamsvleis	[lams·flæjs]
beef	beesvleis	[beəs·flæjs]
rabbit	konynvleis	[konajn·flæjs]

sausage (bologna, pepperoni, etc.)	wors	[vors]
vienna sausage (frankfurter)	Weense worsie	[veɛŋsə vorsi]
bacon	spek	[spek]
ham	ham	[ham]
gammon	gerookte ham	[χeroəktə ham]

pâté	patee	[pateə]
liver	lewer	[levər]
mince (minced meat)	maalvleis	[māl·flæjs]
tongue	tong	[toŋ]

egg	eier	[æjer]
eggs	eiers	[æjers]
egg white	eierwit	[æjer·wit]
egg yolk	dooier	[dojer]

fish	vis	[fis]
seafood	seekos	[seə·kos]
crustaceans	skaaldiere	[skāldirə]
caviar	kaviaar	[kafiār]

crab	krab	[krap]
prawn	garnaal	[χarnāl]
oyster	oester	[ustər]
spiny lobster	seekreef	[seə·kreəf]
octopus	seekat	[seə·kat]
squid	pylinkvis	[pajl·inkfis]

sturgeon	steur	[støər]
salmon	salm	[salm]
halibut	heilbot	[hæjlbot]

cod	kabeljou	[kabeljæʊ]
mackerel	makriel	[makril]
tuna	tuna	[tuna]
eel	paling	[paliŋ]

trout	forel	[forəl]
sardine	sardyn	[sardajn]
pike	varswatersnoek	[farswatər·snuk]
herring	haring	[hariŋ]

bread	brood	[broət]
cheese	kaas	[kās]
sugar	suiker	[sœikər]
salt	sout	[sæʊt]

rice	rys	[rajs]
pasta (macaroni)	pasta	[pasta]
noodles	noedels	[nudɛls]

butter	botter	[bottər]
vegetable oil	plantaardige olie	[plantārdiχə oli]
sunflower oil	sonblomolie	[sonblom·oli]
margarine	margarien	[marχarin]

olives	olywe	[olajvə]
olive oil	olyfolie	[olajf·oli]

milk	melk	[melk]
condensed milk	kondensmelk	[kondɛŋs·melk]
yogurt	jogurt	[joχurt]

| soured cream | suurroom | [sɪr·roəm] |
| cream (of milk) | room | [roəm] |

| mayonnaise | mayonnaise | [majonɛs] |
| buttercream | crème | [krɛm] |

cereal grains (wheat, etc.)	ontbytgraan	[ontbajt·χrān]
flour	meelblom	[meəl·blom]
tinned food	blikkieskos	[blikkis·kos]

cornflakes	mielievlokkies	[mili·flokkis]
honey	heuning	[høəniŋ]
jam	konfyt	[konfajt]
chewing gum	kougom	[kæʊχom]

53. Drinks

water	water	[vatər]
drinking water	drinkwater	[drink·vatər]
mineral water	mineraalwater	[minerāl·vatər]

still (adj)	sonder gas	[sondər χas]
carbonated (adj)	soda-	[soda-]
sparkling (adj)	bruis-	[brœis-]
ice	ys	[ajs]
with ice	met ys	[met ajs]

non-alcoholic (adj)	nie-alkoholies	[ni-alkoholis]
soft drink	koeldrank	[kul·drank]
refreshing drink	verfrissende drank	[ferfrissendə drank]
lemonade	limonade	[limonadə]

spirits	likeure	[likøərə]
wine	wyn	[vajn]
white wine	witwyn	[vit·vajn]
red wine	rooiwyn	[roj·vajn]

liqueur	likeur	[likøər]
champagne	sjampanje	[ʃampanje]
vermouth	vermoet	[fermut]

whisky	whisky	[vhiskaj]
vodka	vodka	[fodka]
gin	jenever	[jenefər]
cognac	brandewyn	[brandə·vajn]
rum	rum	[rum]

coffee	koffie	[koffi]
black coffee	swart koffie	[swart koffi]
white coffee	koffie met melk	[koffi met melk]
cappuccino	capuccino	[kaputʃino]
instant coffee	poeierkoffie	[pujer·koffi]
milk	melk	[melk]
cocktail	mengeldrankie	[menχəl·dranki]

milkshake	melkskommel	[melk·skomməl]
juice	sap	[sap]
tomato juice	tamatiesap	[tamati·sap]
orange juice	lemoensap	[lemoən·sap]
freshly squeezed juice	vars geparste sap	[fars χeparstə sap]

beer	bier	[bir]
lager	ligte bier	[liχtə bir]
bitter	donker bier	[donkər bir]

tea	tee	[teə]
black tea	swart tee	[swart teə]
green tea	groen tee	[χrun teə]

54. Vegetables

| vegetables | groente | [χruntə] |
| greens | groente | [χruntə] |

tomato	tamatie	[tamati]
cucumber	komkommer	[komkommər]
carrot	wortel	[vortəl]
potato	aartappel	[ārtappəl]
onion	ui	[œi]
garlic	knoffel	[knoffəl]

cabbage	kool	[koəl]
cauliflower	blomkool	[blom·koəl]
Brussels sprouts	Brusselspruite	[brussɛl·sprœeitə]
broccoli	broccoli	[brokoli]

beetroot	beet	[beət]
aubergine	eiervrug	[æjerfruχ]
courgette	vingerskorsie	[finər·skorsi]
pumpkin	pampoen	[pampun]
turnip	raap	[rãp]

parsley	pietersielie	[pitərsili]
dill	dille	[dillə]
lettuce	slaai	[slāi]
celery	seldery	[selderaj]

| asparagus | aspersie | [aspersi] |
| spinach | spinasie | [spinasi] |

| pea | ertjie | [ɛrki] |
| beans | boontjies | [boənkis] |

| maize | mielie | [mili] |
| kidney bean | nierboontjie | [nir·boənki] |

sweet paper	paprika	[paprika]
radish	radys	[radajs]
artichoke	artisjok	[artiʃok]

56

55. Fruits. Nuts

fruit	vrugte	[fruχtə]
apple	appel	[appəl]
pear	peer	[peər]
lemon	suurlemoen	[sɪr·lemun]
orange	lemoen	[lemun]
strawberry (garden ~)	aarbei	[ãrbæj]

tangerine	nartjie	[narki]
plum	pruim	[prœim]
peach	perske	[perskə]
apricot	appelkoos	[appɛlkoəs]
raspberry	framboos	[framboəs]
pineapple	pynappel	[pajnappəl]

banana	piesang	[pisaŋ]
watermelon	waatlemoen	[vãtlemun]
grape	druif	[drœif]
cherry	kersie	[kersi]
sour cherry	suurkersie	[sɪr·kersi]
sweet cherry	soetkersie	[sut·kersi]
melon	spanspek	[spaŋspek]

grapefruit	pomelo	[pomelo]
avocado	avokado	[afokado]
papaya	papaja	[papaja]
mango	mango	[manχo]
pomegranate	granaat	[χranãt]

redcurrant	rooi aalbessie	[roj ãlbɛssi]
blackcurrant	swartbessie	[swartbɛssi]
gooseberry	appelliefie	[appɛlifi]
bilberry	bosbessie	[bosbɛssi]
blackberry	braambessie	[brãmbɛssi]

raisin	rosyntjie	[rosajnki]
fig	vy	[faj]
date	dadel	[dadəl]

peanut	grondboontjie	[χront·boənki]
almond	amandel	[amandəl]
walnut	okkerneut	[okkər·nøət]
hazelnut	haselneut	[hasɛl·nøət]
coconut	klapper	[klappər]
pistachios	pistachio	[pistatʃio]

56. Bread. Sweets

bakers' confectionery (pastry)	soet gebak	[sut χebak]
bread	brood	[broət]
biscuits	koekies	[kukis]
chocolate (n)	sjokolade	[ʃokoladə]

chocolate (as adj)	sjokolade	[ʃokoladə]
candy (wrapped)	lekkers	[lɛkkərs]
cake (e.g. cupcake)	koek	[kuk]
cake (e.g. birthday ~)	koek	[kuk]

| pie (e.g. apple ~) | pastei | [pastæj] |
| filling (for cake, pie) | vulsel | [fulsəl] |

jam (whole fruit jam)	konfyt	[konfajt]
marmalade	marmelade	[marmeladə]
waffles	wafels	[vafɛls]
ice-cream	roomys	[roəm·ajs]
pudding (Christmas ~)	poeding	[pudiŋ]

57. Spices

salt	sout	[sæʊt]
salty (adj)	sout	[sæʊt]
to salt (vt)	sout	[sæʊt]

black pepper	swart peper	[swart pepər]
red pepper (milled ~)	rooi peper	[roj pepər]
mustard	mosterd	[mostert]
horseradish	peperwortel	[peper·wortəl]

condiment	smaakmiddel	[smāk·middəl]
spice	spesery	[spesəraj]
sauce	sous	[sæʊs]
vinegar	asyn	[asajn]

anise	anys	[anajs]
basil	basilikum	[basilikum]
cloves	naeltjies	[naɛlkis]
ginger	gemmer	[χɛmmər]
coriander	koljander	[koljandər]
cinnamon	kaneel	[kaneəl]

sesame	sesamsaad	[sesam·sāt]
bay leaf	lourierblaar	[læʊrir·blār]
paprika	paprika	[paprika]
caraway	komynsaad	[komajnsāt]
saffron	saffraan	[saffrān]

PERSONAL INFORMATION. FAMILY

58. Personal information. Forms

name (first name)	voornaam	[foərnām]
surname (last name)	van	[fan]
date of birth	geboortedatum	[χeboərtə·datum]
place of birth	geboorteplek	[χeboərtə·plek]
nationality	nasionaliteit	[naʃionalitæjt]
place of residence	woonplek	[voən·plek]
country	land	[lant]
profession (occupation)	beroep	[berup]
gender, sex	geslag	[χeslaχ]
height	lengte	[leŋtə]
weight	gewig	[χeveχ]

59. Family members. Relatives

mother	moeder	[mudər]
father	vader	[fɑdor]
son	seun	[søən]
daughter	dogter	[doχtər]
younger daughter	jonger dogter	[joŋər doχtər]
younger son	jonger seun	[joŋər søən]
eldest daughter	oudste dogter	[æudstə doχtər]
eldest son	oudste seun	[æudstə søən]
brother	broer	[brur]
elder brother	ouer broer	[æuer brur]
younger brother	jonger broer	[joŋər brur]
sister	suster	[sustər]
elder sister	ouer suster	[æuer sustər]
younger sister	jonger suster	[joŋər sustər]
cousin (masc.)	neef	[neəf]
cousin (fem.)	neef	[neəf]
mummy	ma	[ma]
dad, daddy	pa	[pa]
parents	ouers	[æuers]
child	kind	[kint]
children	kinders	[kindərs]
grandmother	ouma	[æuma]
grandfather	oupa	[æupa]

grandson	kleinseun	[klæjn·søən]
granddaughter	kleindogter	[klæjn·doχtər]
grandchildren	kleinkinders	[klæjn·kindərs]

uncle	oom	[oəm]
aunt	tante	[tantə]
nephew	neef	[neəf]
niece	nig	[niχ]

mother-in-law (wife's mother)	skoonma	[skoən·ma]
father-in-law (husband's father)	skoonpa	[skoən·pa]
son-in-law (daughter's husband)	skoonseun	[skoən·søən]
stepmother	stiefma	[stifma]
stepfather	stiefpa	[stifpa]

infant	baba	[baba]
baby (infant)	baba	[baba]
little boy, kid	seuntjie	[søənki]

wife	vrou	[fræʊ]
husband	man	[man]
spouse (husband)	eggenoot	[ɛχχenoət]
spouse (wife)	eggenote	[ɛχχenotə]

married (masc.)	getroud	[χetræʊt]
married (fem.)	getroud	[χetræʊt]
single (unmarried)	ongetroud	[onχətræʊt]
bachelor	vrygesel	[frajχesəl]
divorced (masc.)	geskei	[χeskæj]
widow	weduwee	[veduveə]
widower	wedunaar	[vedunãr]

relative	familielid	[famililit]
close relative	na familie	[na famili]
distant relative	ver familie	[fer famili]
relatives	familielede	[famililedə]

orphan (boy or girl)	weeskind	[veəskint]
guardian (of a minor)	voog	[foəχ]
to adopt (a boy)	aanneem	[ānneəm]
to adopt (a girl)	aanneem	[ānneəm]

60. Friends. Colleagues

friend (masc.)	vriend	[frint]
friend (fem.)	vriendin	[frindin]
friendship	vriendskap	[frindskap]
to be friends	bevriend wees	[befrint veəs]

| pal (masc.) | maat | [mãt] |
| pal (fem.) | vriendin | [frindin] |

partner	maat	[mãt]
chief (boss)	baas	[bãs]
superior (n)	baas	[bãs]
owner, proprietor	eienaar	[æjenãr]
subordinate (n)	ondergeskikte	[ondərχeskiktə]
colleague	kollega	[kolleχa]

acquaintance (person)	kennis	[kɛnnis]
fellow traveller	medereisiger	[medə·ræjsiχər]
classmate	klasmaat	[klas·mãt]

neighbour (masc.)	buurman	[bɪrman]
neighbour (fem.)	buurvrou	[bɪrfræʊ]
neighbours	bure	[burə]

HUMAN BODY. MEDICINE

61. Head

head	kop	[kop]
face	gesig	[χesəχ]
nose	neus	[nøəs]
mouth	mond	[mont]
eye	oog	[oəχ]
eyes	oë	[oε]
pupil	pupil	[pupil]
eyebrow	wenkbrou	[vεnk·bræʊ]
eyelash	ooghaar	[oəχ·hãr]
eyelid	ooglid	[oəχ·lit]
tongue	tong	[toŋ]
tooth	tand	[tant]
lips	lippe	[lippə]
cheekbones	wangbene	[vaŋ·benə]
gum	tandvleis	[tand·flæjs]
palate	verhemelte	[fer·hemεltə]
nostrils	neusgate	[nøəsχatə]
chin	ken	[ken]
jaw	kakebeen	[kakebeən]
cheek	wang	[vaŋ]
forehead	voorhoof	[foərhoəf]
temple	slaap	[slãp]
ear	oor	[oər]
back of the head	agterkop	[aχtərkop]
neck	nek	[nek]
throat	keel	[keəl]
hair	haar	[hãr]
hairstyle	kapsel	[kapsəl]
haircut	haarstyl	[hãrstajl]
wig	pruik	[prœik]
moustache	snor	[snor]
beard	baard	[bãrt]
to have (a beard, etc.)	dra	[dra]
plait	vlegsel	[fleχsəl]
sideboards	bakkebaarde	[bakkəbãrdə]
red-haired (adj)	rooiharig	[roj·harəχ]
grey (hair)	grys	[χrajs]
bald (adj)	kaal	[kãl]
bald patch	kaal plek	[kãl plek]

| ponytail | poniestert | [poni·stert] |
| fringe | gordyntjiekapsel | [χordajnki·kapsəl] |

62. Human body

| hand | hand | [hant] |
| arm | arm | [arm] |

finger	vinger	[fiŋər]
toe	toon	[toən]
thumb	duim	[dœim]
little finger	pinkie	[pinki]
nail	nael	[naəl]

fist	vuis	[fœis]
palm	palm	[palm]
wrist	pols	[pols]
forearm	voorarm	[foərarm]
elbow	elmboog	[εlmboəχ]
shoulder	skouer	[skæʊər]

leg	been	[beən]
foot	voet	[fut]
knee	knie	[kni]
calf (part of leg)	kuit	[kœit]
hip	heup	[høəp]
heel	hakskeen	[hak·skeən]

body	liggaam	[liχχām]
stomach	maag	[māχ]
chest	bors	[bors]
breast	bors	[bors]
flank	sy	[saj]
back	rug	[ruχ]
lower back	lae rug	[laə ruχ]
waist	middel	[middəl]

navel (belly button)	naeltjie	[naεlki]
buttocks	boude	[bæʊdə]
bottom	sitvlak	[sitflak]

beauty spot	moesie	[musi]
birthmark (café au lait spot)	moedervlek	[mudər·flek]
tattoo	tatoe	[tatu]
scar	litteken	[littekən]

63. Diseases

illness	siekte	[siktə]
to be ill	siek wees	[sik veəs]
health	gesondheid	[χesonthæjt]
runny nose (coryza)	loopneus	[loəpnøəs]

| tonsillitis | keelontsteking | [keəl·ontstekiŋ] |
| cold (illness) | verkoue | [ferkæuə] |

bronchitis	bronchitis	[bronχitis]
pneumonia	longontsteking	[loŋ·ontstekiŋ]
flu, influenza	griep	[χrip]

shortsighted (adj)	bysiende	[bajsində]
longsighted (adj)	versiende	[fersində]
strabismus (crossed eyes)	skeelheid	[skeəlhæjt]
squint-eyed (adj)	skeel	[skeəl]
cataract	katarak	[katarak]
glaucoma	gloukoom	[χlæukoəm]

stroke	beroerte	[berurtə]
heart attack	hartaanval	[hart·ãnfal]
myocardial infarction	hartinfark	[hart·infark]
paralysis	verlamming	[ferlammiŋ]
to paralyse (vt)	verlam	[ferlam]

allergy	allergie	[allerχi]
asthma	asma	[asma]
diabetes	suikersiekte	[sœikər·siktə]

| toothache | tandpyn | [tand·pajn] |
| caries | tandbederf | [tand·bederf] |

diarrhoea	diarree	[diarreə]
constipation	hardlywigheid	[hardlajviχæjt]
stomach upset	maagongesteldheid	[mãχ·oŋəstɛldhæjt]
food poisoning	voedselvergiftiging	[fudsəl·ferχiftəχiŋ]
to get food poisoning	voedselvergiftiging kry	[fudsəl·ferχiftəχiŋ kraj]

arthritis	artritis	[artritis]
rickets	Engelse siekte	[ɛŋəlsə siktə]
rheumatism	reumatiek	[røəmatik]
atherosclerosis	artrosklerose	[artrosklerosə]

gastritis	maagontsteking	[mãχ·ontstekiŋ]
appendicitis	blindedermontsteking	[blindəderm·ontstekiŋ]
cholecystitis	galblaasontsteking	[χalblãs·ontstekiŋ]
ulcer	maagsweer	[mãχsweər]

measles	masels	[masɛls]
rubella (German measles)	Duitse masels	[dœitsə masɛls]
jaundice	geelsug	[χeəlsuχ]
hepatitis	hepatitis	[hepatitis]

schizophrenia	skisofrenie	[skisofreni]
rabies (hydrophobia)	hondsdolheid	[hondsdolhæjt]
neurosis	neurose	[nøərosə]
concussion	harsingskudding	[harsiŋ·skuddiŋ]

cancer	kanker	[kankər]
sclerosis	sklerose	[sklerosə]
multiple sclerosis	veelvuldige sklerose	[feəlfuldiχə sklerosə]

alcoholism	**alkoholisme**	[alkoholismə]
alcoholic (n)	**alkoholikus**	[alkoholikus]
syphilis	**sifilis**	[sifilis]
AIDS	**VIGS**	[vigs]
tumour	**tumor**	[tumor]
malignant (adj)	**kwaadaardig**	[kwādārdəχ]
benign (adj)	**goedaardig**	[χudārdəχ]
fever	**koors**	[koərs]
malaria	**malaria**	[malaria]
gangrene	**gangreen**	[χanχreən]
seasickness	**seesiekte**	[seə·siktə]
epilepsy	**epilepsie**	[ɛpilepsi]
epidemic	**epidemie**	[ɛpidemi]
typhus	**tifus**	[tifus]
tuberculosis	**tuberkulose**	[tuberkulosə]
cholera	**cholera**	[χolera]
plague (bubonic ~)	**pes**	[pes]

64. Symptoms. Treatments. Part 1

symptom	**simptoom**	[simptoəm]
temperature	**temperatuur**	[temperatɪr]
high temperature (fever)	**koors**	[koərs]
pulse	**polsslag**	[pols·slaχ]
dizziness (vertigo)	**duiseligheid**	[dœiseliχæjt]
hot (adj)	**warm**	[varm]
shivering	**koue rillings**	[kæʊə rilliŋs]
pale (e.g. ~ face)	**bleek**	[bleək]
cough	**hoes**	[hus]
to cough (vi)	**hoes**	[hus]
to sneeze (vi)	**nies**	[nis]
faint	**floute**	[flæʊtə]
to faint (vi)	**flou word**	[flæʊ vort]
bruise (hématome)	**blou kol**	[blæʊ kol]
bump (lump)	**knop**	[knop]
to bang (bump)	**stamp**	[stamp]
contusion (bruise)	**besering**	[beseriŋ]
to limp (vi)	**hink**	[hink]
dislocation	**ontwrigting**	[ontwriχtiŋ]
to dislocate (vt)	**ontwrig**	[ontwrəχ]
fracture	**breuk**	[brøək]
to have a fracture	**n breuk hè**	[n brøək hɛ:]
cut (e.g. paper ~)	**sny**	[snaj]
to cut oneself	**jouself sny**	[jæʊsɛlf snaj]
bleeding	**bloeding**	[bludiŋ]
burn (injury)	**brandwond**	[brant·vont]

to get burned	jouself brand	[jæusɛlf brant]
to prick (vt)	prik	[prik]
to prick oneself	jouself prik	[jæusɛlf prik]
to injure (vt)	seermaak	[seərmãk]
injury	besering	[beseriŋ]
wound	wond	[vont]
trauma	trauma	[trɔuma]

to be delirious	yl	[ajl]
to stutter (vi)	stotter	[stottər]
sunstroke	sonsteek	[sɔŋ·steək]

65. Symptoms. Treatments. Part 2

| pain, ache | pyn | [pajn] |
| splinter (in foot, etc.) | splinter | [splintər] |

sweat (perspiration)	sweet	[sweət]
to sweat (perspire)	sweet	[sweət]
vomiting	braak	[brãk]
convulsions	stuiptrekkings	[stœip·trɛkkiŋs]

pregnant (adj)	swanger	[swaŋər]
to be born	gebore word	[χeborə vort]
delivery, labour	geboorte	[χeboərtə]
to deliver (~ a baby)	baar	[bãr]
abortion	aborsie	[aborsi]

breathing, respiration	asemhaling	[asemhaliŋ]
in-breath (inhalation)	inaseming	[inasemiŋ]
out-breath (exhalation)	uitaseming	[œitasemiŋ]
to exhale (breathe out)	uitasem	[œitasem]
to inhale (vi)	inasem	[inasem]

disabled person	invalide	[infalidə]
cripple	kreupel	[krøəpəl]
drug addict	dwelmslaaf	[dwɛlm·slãf]

deaf (adj)	doof	[doəf]
mute (adj)	stom	[stom]
deaf mute (adj)	doofstom	[doəf·stom]

mad, insane (adj)	swaksinnig	[swaksinnəχ]
madman (demented person)	kranksinnige	[kranksinniχə]
madwoman	kranksinnige	[kranksinniχə]
to go insane	kranksinnig word	[kranksinnəχ vort]

gene	geen	[χeən]
immunity	immuniteit	[immunitæjt]
hereditary (adj)	erflik	[ɛrflik]
congenital (adj)	aangebore	[ãnχəborə]
virus	virus	[firus]
microbe	mikrobe	[mikrobə]

bacterium	**bakterie**	[bakteri]
infection	**infeksie**	[infeksi]

66. Symptoms. Treatments. Part 3

hospital	**hospitaal**	[hospitāl]
patient	**pasiënt**	[pasiɛnt]
diagnosis	**diagnose**	[diaχnosə]
cure	**genesing**	[χenesiŋ]
medical treatment	**mediese behandeling**	[medisə behandəliŋ]
to get treatment	**behandeling kry**	[behandəliŋ kraj]
to treat (~ a patient)	**behandel**	[behandəl]
to nurse (look after)	**versorg**	[fersorχ]
care (nursing ~)	**versorging**	[fersorχiŋ]
operation, surgery	**operasie**	[operasi]
to bandage (head, limb)	**verbind**	[ferbint]
bandaging	**verband**	[ferbant]
vaccination	**inenting**	[inɛntiŋ]
to vaccinate (vt)	**inent**	[inɛnt]
injection	**inspuiting**	[inspœitiŋ]
attack	**aanval**	[ānfal]
amputation	**amputasie**	[amputasi]
to amputate (vt)	**amputeer**	[amputeər]
coma	**koma**	[koma]
intensive care	**intensiewe sorg**	[intɛnsivə sorχ]
to recover (~ from flu)	**herstel**	[herstəl]
condition (patient's ~)	**kondisie**	[kondisi]
consciousness	**bewussyn**	[bevussajn]
memory (faculty)	**geheue**	[χəhøə]
to pull out (tooth)	**trek**	[trek]
filling	**vulsel**	[fulsəl]
to fill (a tooth)	**vul**	[ful]
hypnosis	**hipnose**	[hipnosə]
to hypnotize (vt)	**hipnotiseer**	[hipnotiseər]

67. Medicine. Drugs. Accessories

medicine, drug	**medisyn**	[medisajn]
remedy	**geneesmiddel**	[χeneəs·middəl]
to prescribe (vt)	**voorskryf**	[foərskrajf]
prescription	**voorskrif**	[foərskrif]
tablet, pill	**pil**	[pil]
ointment	**salf**	[salf]
ampoule	**ampul**	[ampul]

mixture	**mengsel**	[meŋsəl]
syrup	**stroop**	[stroəp]
pill	**pil**	[pil]
powder	**poeier**	[pujer]

gauze bandage	**verband**	[ferbant]
cotton wool	**watte**	[vattə]
iodine	**iodium**	[iodium]

plaster	**pleister**	[plæjstər]
eyedropper	**oogdrupper**	[oeχ·druppər]
thermometer	**termometer**	[termometər]
syringe	**spuitnaald**	[spœit·nǎlt]

wheelchair	**rolstoel**	[rol·stul]
crutches	**krukke**	[krukkə]

painkiller	**pynstiller**	[pajn·stillər]
laxative	**lakseermiddel**	[lakseer·middəl]
spirits (ethanol)	**spiritus**	[spiritus]
medicinal herbs	**geneeskragtige kruie**	[χeneəs·kraχtiχə krœiə]
herbal (~ tea)	**kruie-**	[krœie-]

FLAT

68. Flat

flat	woonstel	[voəŋstəl]
room	kamer	[kamər]
bedroom	slaapkamer	[slāp·kamər]
dining room	eetkamer	[eet·kamər]
living room	sitkamer	[sit·kamər]
study (home office)	studeerkamer	[studeər·kamər]
entry room	ingangsportaal	[inχaŋs·portāl]
bathroom	badkamer	[bad·kamər]
water closet	toilet	[tojlet]
ceiling	plafon	[plafon]
floor	vloer	[flur]
corner	hoek	[huk]

69. Furniture. Interior

furniture	meubels	[møəbɛls]
table	tafel	[tafel]
chair	stoel	[stul]
bed	bed	[bet]
sofa, settee	rusbank	[rusbank]
armchair	gemakstoel	[χemak·stul]
bookcase	boekkas	[buk·kas]
shelf	rak	[rak]
wardrobe	klerekas	[klerə·kas]
coat rack (wall-mounted ~)	kapstok	[kapstok]
coat stand	kapstok	[kapstok]
chest of drawers	laaikas	[lājkas]
coffee table	koffietafel	[koffi·tafəl]
mirror	spieêl	[spiɛl]
carpet	mat	[mat]
small carpet	matjie	[maki]
fireplace	vuurherd	[fɪr·hert]
candle	kers	[kers]
candlestick	kandelaar	[kandelār]
drapes	gordyne	[χordajnə]
wallpaper	muurpapier	[mɪr·papir]

blinds (jalousie)	blindings	[blindiŋs]
table lamp	tafellamp	[tafel·lamp]
wall lamp (sconce)	muurlamp	[mɪr·lamp]
standard lamp	staanlamp	[stān·lamp]
chandelier	kroonlugter	[kroən·luχtər]

leg (of chair, table)	poot	[poət]
armrest	armleuning	[arm·løəniŋ]
back (backrest)	rugleuning	[ruχ·løəniŋ]
drawer	laai	[lāi]

70. Bedding

bedclothes	beddegoed	[beddə·χut]
pillow	kussing	[kussiŋ]
pillowslip	kussingsloop	[kussiŋ·sloəp]
duvet	duvet	[dufet]
sheet	laken	[laken]
bedspread	bedsprei	[bed·spræj]

71. Kitchen

kitchen	kombuis	[kombœis]
gas	gas	[χas]
gas cooker	gasstoof	[χas·stoəf]
electric cooker	elektriese stoof	[elektrisə stoəf]
oven	oond	[oent]
microwave oven	mikrogolfoond	[mikroχolf·oent]

refrigerator	yskas	[ajs·kas]
freezer	vrieskas	[friskas]
dishwasher	skottelgoedwasser	[skottɛlχud·wassər]

mincer	vleismeul	[flæjs·møəl]
juicer	versapper	[fersappər]
toaster	broodrooster	[broəd·roəstər]
mixer	menger	[meŋər]

coffee machine	koffiemasjien	[koffi·maʃin]
coffee pot	koffiepot	[koffi·pot]
coffee grinder	koffiemeul	[koffi·møəl]

kettle	fluitketel	[flœit·ketəl]
teapot	teepot	[teə·pot]
lid	deksel	[deksəl]
tea strainer	teesiffie	[teə·siffi]

spoon	lepel	[lepəl]
teaspoon	teelepeltjie	[teə·lepəlki]
soup spoon	soplepel	[sop·lepəl]
fork	vurk	[furk]
knife	mes	[mes]

tableware (dishes)	**tafelgerei**	[tafel·χeræj]
plate (dinner ~)	**bord**	[bort]
saucer	**piering**	[piriŋ]

shot glass	**likeurglas**	[likøər·χlas]
glass (tumbler)	**glas**	[χlas]
cup	**koppie**	[koppi]

sugar bowl	**suikerpot**	[sœikər·pot]
salt cellar	**soutvaatjie**	[sæʊt·fāki]
pepper pot	**pepervaatjie**	[pepər·fāki]
butter dish	**botterbakkie**	[bottər·bakki]

stock pot (soup pot)	**soppot**	[sop·pot]
frying pan (skillet)	**braaipan**	[brāj·pan]
ladle	**opskeplepel**	[opskep·lepəl]
colander	**vergiet**	[ferχit]
tray (serving ~)	**skinkbord**	[skink·bort]

bottle	**bottel**	[bottəl]
jar (glass)	**fles**	[fles]
tin (can)	**blikkie**	[blikki]

bottle opener	**botteloopmaker**	[bottəl·oəpmakər]
tin opener	**blikoopmaker**	[blik·oəpmakər]
corkscrew	**kurktrekker**	[kurk·trɛkkər]
filter	**filter**	[filtər]
to filter (vt)	**filter**	[filtər]

waste (food ~, etc.)	**vullis**	[fullis]
waste bin (kitchen ~)	**vullisbak**	[fullis·bak]

72. Bathroom

bathroom	**badkamer**	[bad·kamər]
water	**water**	[vatər]
tap	**kraan**	[krān]
hot water	**warme water**	[varmə vatər]
cold water	**koue water**	[kæʊə vatər]

toothpaste	**tandepasta**	[tandə·pasta]
to clean one's teeth	**tande borsel**	[tandə borsəl]
toothbrush	**tandeborsel**	[tandə·borsəl]

to shave (vi)	**skeer**	[skeər]
shaving foam	**skeerroom**	[skeər·roəm]
razor	**skeermes**	[skeər·mes]

to wash (one's hands, etc.)	**was**	[vas]
to have a bath	**bad**	[bat]
shower	**stort**	[stort]
to have a shower	**stort**	[stort]
bath	**bad**	[bat]
toilet (toilet bowl)	**toilet**	[tojlet]

sink (washbasin)	wasbak	[vas·bak]
soap	seep	[seəp]
soap dish	seepbakkie	[seəp·bakki]

sponge	spons	[spɔŋs]
shampoo	sjampoe	[ʃampu]
towel	handdoek	[handduk]
bathrobe	badjas	[batjas]

laundry (process)	was	[vas]
washing machine	wasmasjien	[vas·maʃin]
to do the laundry	die wasgoed was	[di vasχut vas]
washing powder	waspoeier	[vas·pujer]

73. Household appliances

TV, telly	TV-stel	[te·fe-stəl]
tape recorder	bandspeler	[band·speler]
video	videomasjien	[video·maʃin]
radio	radio	[radio]
player (CD, MP3, etc.)	speler	[speler]

video projector	videoprojektor	[video·projektor]
home cinema	tuisfliekteater	[tœis·flik·teater]
DVD player	DVD-speler	[de·fe·de-speler]
amplifier	versterker	[fersterker]
video game console	videokonsole	[video·kɔŋsole]

video camera	videokamera	[video·kamera]
camera (photo)	kamera	[kamera]
digital camera	digitale kamera	[diχitale kamera]

vacuum cleaner	stofsuier	[stof·sœier]
iron (e.g. steam ~)	strykyster	[strajk·ajster]
ironing board	strykplank	[strajk·plank]

telephone	telefoon	[telefoən]
mobile phone	selfoon	[sɛlfoən]
typewriter	tikmasjien	[tik·maʃin]
sewing machine	naaimasjien	[naj·maʃin]

microphone	mikrofoon	[mikrofoən]
headphones	koptelefoon	[kop·telefoən]
remote control (TV)	afstandsbeheer	[afstands·beheər]

CD, compact disc	CD	[se·de]
cassette, tape	kasset	[kasset]
vinyl record	plaat	[plāt]

THE EARTH. WEATHER

74. Outer space

space	kosmos	[kosmos]
space (as adj)	kosmies	[kosmis]
outer space	buitenste ruimte	[bœitɛŋstə rajmtə]
world	wêreld	[værɛlt]
universe	heelal	[heəlal]
galaxy	sterrestelsel	[sterrə·stɛlsəl]
star	ster	[ster]
constellation	sterrebeeld	[sterrə·beəlt]
planet	planeet	[planeət]
satellite	satelliet	[satɛllit]
meteorite	meteoriet	[meteorit]
comet	komeet	[komeət]
asteroid	asteroïed	[asteroïət]
orbit	baan	[bãn]
to revolve	draai	[drãi]
(~ around the Earth)		
atmosphere	atmosfeer	[atmosfeər]
the Sun	die Son	[di son]
solar system	sonnestelsel	[sonnə·stɛlsəl]
solar eclipse	sonsverduistering	[soŋs·ferdœisteriŋ]
the Earth	die Aarde	[di ãrdə]
the Moon	die Maan	[di mãn]
Mars	Mars	[mars]
Venus	Venus	[fenus]
Jupiter	Jupiter	[jupitər]
Saturn	Saturnus	[saturnus]
Mercury	Mercurius	[merkurius]
Uranus	Uranus	[uranus]
Neptune	Neptunus	[neptunus]
Pluto	Pluto	[pluto]
Milky Way	Melkweg	[melk·weχ]
Great Bear (Ursa Major)	Groot Beer	[χroət beər]
North Star	Poolster	[poəl·stər]
Martian	marsbewoner	[mars·bevonər]
extraterrestrial (n)	buiteaardse wese	[bœitə·ãrdsə vesə]
alien	ruimtewese	[rœimtə·vesə]

flying saucer	vlieënde skottel	[fliɛndə skottəl]
spaceship	ruimteskip	[rœimtə·skip]
space station	ruimtestasie	[rœimtə·stasi]
blast-off	vertrek	[fertrek]

engine	enjin	[ɛndʒin]
nozzle	uitlaatpyp	[œitlãt·pajp]
fuel	brandstof	[brantstof]

| cockpit, flight deck | stuurkajuit | [stɪr·kajœit] |
| aerial | lugdraad | [luχdrãt] |

porthole	patryspoort	[patrajs·poərt]
solar panel	sonpaneel	[son·paneəl]
spacesuit	ruimtepak	[rœimtə·pak]

| weightlessness | gewigloosheid | [χeviχloəshæjt] |
| oxygen | suurstof | [sɪrstof] |

| docking (in space) | koppeling | [koppeliŋ] |
| to dock (vi, vt) | koppel | [koppəl] |

| observatory | observatorium | [observatorium] |
| telescope | teleskoop | [teleskoəp] |

| to observe (vt) | waarneem | [vãrneəm] |
| to explore (vt) | eksploreer | [ɛksploreər] |

75. The Earth

the Earth	die Aarde	[di ãrdə]
the globe (the Earth)	die aardbol	[di ãrdbol]
planet	planeet	[planeət]

atmosphere	atmosfeer	[atmosfeər]
geography	geografie	[χeoχrafi]
nature	natuur	[natɪr]

globe (table ~)	aardbol	[ãrd·bol]
map	kaart	[kãrt]
atlas	atlas	[atlas]

| Europe | Europa | [øəropa] |
| Asia | Asië | [asiɛ] |

| Africa | Afrika | [afrika] |
| Australia | Australië | [ɔustraliɛ] |

America	Amerika	[amerika]
North America	Noord-Amerika	[noərd-amerika]
South America	Suid-Amerika	[sœid-amerika]

| Antarctica | Suidpool | [sœid·poəl] |
| the Arctic | Noordpool | [noərd·poəl] |

76. Cardinal directions

north	noorde	[noərdə]
to the north	na die noorde	[na di noərdə]
in the north	in die noorde	[in di noərdə]
northern (adj)	noordelik	[noərdəlik]
south	suide	[sœidə]
to the south	na die suide	[na di sœidə]
in the south	in die suide	[in di sœidə]
southern (adj)	suidelik	[sœidəlik]
west	weste	[vestə]
to the west	na die weste	[na di vestə]
in the west	in die weste	[in di vestə]
western (adj)	westelik	[vestəlik]
east	ooste	[oəstə]
to the east	na die ooste	[na di oəstə]
in the east	in die ooste	[in di oəstə]
eastern (adj)	oostelik	[oəstəlik]

77. Sea. Ocean

sea	see	[seə]
ocean	oseaan	[oseãn]
gulf (bay)	golf	[χolf]
straits	straat	[strãt]
land (solid ground)	land	[lant]
continent (mainland)	kontinent	[kontinent]
island	eiland	[æjlant]
peninsula	skiereiland	[skir·æjlant]
archipelago	argipel	[arχipəl]
bay, cove	baai	[bãi]
harbour	hawe	[havə]
lagoon	strandmeer	[strand·meer]
cape	kaap	[kãp]
atoll	atol	[atol]
reef	rif	[rif]
coral	koraal	[korãl]
coral reef	koraalrif	[korãl·rif]
deep (adj)	diep	[dip]
depth (deep water)	diepte	[diptə]
abyss	afgrond	[afχront]
trench (e.g. Mariana ~)	trog	[troχ]
current (Ocean ~)	stroming	[stromiŋ]
to surround (bathe)	omring	[omriŋ]

| shore | oewer | [uvər] |
| coast | kus | [kus] |

flow (flood tide)	hoogwater	[hoəχ·vatər]
ebb (ebb tide)	laagwater	[lāχ·vatər]
shoal	sandbank	[sand·bank]
bottom (~ of the sea)	bodem	[bodem]

wave	golf	[χolf]
crest (~ of a wave)	kruin	[krœin]
spume (sea foam)	skuim	[skœim]

storm (sea storm)	storm	[storm]
hurricane	orkaan	[orkān]
tsunami	tsunami	[tsunami]
calm (dead ~)	windstilte	[vindstiltə]
quiet, calm (adj)	kalm	[kalm]

| pole | pool | [poəl] |
| polar (adj) | polêr | [polær] |

latitude	breedtegraad	[breədtə·χrāt]
longitude	lengtegraad	[leŋtə·χrāt]
parallel	parallel	[paralləl]
equator	ewenaar	[ɛvenār]

sky	hemel	[heməl]
horizon	horison	[horison]
air	lug	[luχ]

lighthouse	vuurtoring	[fɪrtoriŋ]
to dive (vi)	duik	[dœik]
to sink (ab. boat)	sink	[sink]
treasures	skatte	[skattə]

78. Seas & Oceans names

Atlantic Ocean	Atlantiese oseaan	[atlantisə oseān]
Indian Ocean	Indiese Oseaan	[indisə oseān]
Pacific Ocean	Stille Oseaan	[stillə oseān]
Arctic Ocean	Noordelike Yssee	[noərdelikə ajs·seə]

Black Sea	Swart See	[swart seə]
Red Sea	Rooi See	[roj seə]
Yellow Sea	Geel See	[χeəl seə]
White Sea	Witsee	[vit·seə]

Caspian Sea	Kaspiese See	[kaspisə seə]
Dead Sea	Dooie See	[doje seə]
Mediterranean Sea	Middellandse See	[middəllandsə seə]

Aegean Sea	Egeïese See	[ɛχejesə seə]
Adriatic Sea	Adriatiese See	[adriatisə seə]
Arabian Sea	Arabiese See	[arabisə seə]

Sea of Japan	**Japanse See**	[japaŋsə see]
Bering Sea	**Beringsee**	[beriŋ·see]
South China Sea	**Suid-Sjinese See**	[sœid-ʃinesə see]
Coral Sea	**Koraalsee**	[korāl·see]
Tasman Sea	**Tasmansee**	[tasmaŋ·see]
Caribbean Sea	**Karibiese See**	[karibisə see]
Barents Sea	**Barentssee**	[barents·see]
Kara Sea	**Karasee**	[kara·see]
North Sea	**Noordsee**	[noərd·see]
Baltic Sea	**Baltiese See**	[baltisə see]
Norwegian Sea	**Noorse See**	[noərsə see]

79. Mountains

mountain	**berg**	[berχ]
mountain range	**bergreeks**	[berχ·reəks]
mountain ridge	**bergrug**	[berχ·ruχ]
summit, top	**top**	[top]
peak	**piek**	[pik]
foot (~ of the mountain)	**voet**	[fut]
slope (mountainside)	**helling**	[hɛlliŋ]
volcano	**vulkaan**	[fulkān]
active volcano	**aktiewe vulkaan**	[aktivo fulkān]
dormant volcano	**rustende vulkaan**	[rustendə fulkān]
eruption	**uitbarsting**	[œitbarstiŋ]
crater	**krater**	[kratər]
magma	**magma**	[maχma]
lava	**lawa**	[lava]
molten (~ lava)	**gloeiende**	[χlujendə]
canyon	**diepkloof**	[dip·kloəf]
gorge	**kloof**	[kloəf]
crevice	**skeur**	[skøər]
abyss (chasm)	**afgrond**	[afχront]
pass, col	**bergpas**	[berχ·pas]
plateau	**plato**	[plato]
cliff	**krans**	[kraŋs]
hill	**kop**	[kop]
glacier	**gletser**	[χletsər]
waterfall	**waterval**	[vatər·fal]
geyser	**geiser**	[χæjsər]
lake	**meer**	[meər]
plain	**vlakte**	[flaktə]
landscape	**landskap**	[landskap]
echo	**eggo**	[ɛχχo]

alpinist	alpinis	[alpinis]
rock climber	bergklimmer	[berχ·klimmər]
to conquer (in climbing)	baasraak	[bāsrāk]
climb (an easy ~)	beklimming	[beklimmiŋ]

80. Mountains names

The Alps	die Alpe	[di alpə]
Mont Blanc	Mont Blanc	[mon blan]
The Pyrenees	die Pireneë	[di pireneɛ]

The Carpathians	die Karpate	[di karpatə]
The Ural Mountains	die Oeralgebergte	[di ural·χəberχtə]
The Caucasus Mountains	die Koukasus Gebergte	[di kæʊkasus χəberχtə]
Mount Elbrus	Elbroes	[ɛlbrus]

The Altai Mountains	die Altai-gebergte	[di altaj-χəberχtə]
The Tian Shan	die Tian Shan	[di tian ʃan]
The Pamir Mountains	die Pamir	[di pamir]
The Himalayas	die Himalajas	[di himalajas]
Mount Everest	Everest	[ɛverest]

| The Andes | die Andes | [di andes] |
| Mount Kilimanjaro | Kilimanjaro | [kilimandʒaro] |

81. Rivers

river	rivier	[rifir]
spring (natural source)	bron	[bron]
riverbed (river channel)	rivierbed	[rifir·bet]
basin (river valley)	stroomgebied	[stroəm·χebit]
to flow into ...	uitmond in ...	[œitmont in ...]

| tributary | syrivier | [saj·rifir] |
| bank (of river) | oewer | [uvər] |

current (stream)	stroming	[stromiŋ]
downstream (adv)	stroomafwaarts	[stroəm·afvārts]
upstream (adv)	stroomopwaarts	[stroəm·opvārts]

inundation	oorstroming	[oərstromiŋ]
flooding	oorstroming	[oərstromiŋ]
to overflow (vi)	oor sy walle loop	[oər saj vallə loəp]
to flood (vt)	oorstroom	[oərstroəm]

| shallow (shoal) | sandbank | [sand·bank] |
| rapids | stroomversnellings | [stroəm·fersnɛlliŋs] |

dam	damwal	[dam·wal]
canal	kanaal	[kanāl]
reservoir (artificial lake)	opgaardam	[opχār·dam]
sluice, lock	sluis	[slœis]

water body (pond, etc.)	dam	[dam]
swamp (marshland)	moeras	[muras]
bog, marsh	vlei	[flæj]
whirlpool	draaikolk	[drāj·kolk]

stream (brook)	spruit	[sprœit]
drinking (ab. water)	drink-	[drink-]
fresh (~ water)	vars	[fars]

ice	ys	[ajs]
to freeze over (ab. river, etc.)	bevries	[befris]

82. Rivers names

Seine	Seine	[sæjn]
Loire	Loire	[lua:r]

Thames	Teems	[tems]
Rhine	Ryn	[rajn]
Danube	Donau	[donɔu]

Volga	Wolga	[volga]
Don	Don	[don]
Lena	Lena	[lena]

Yellow River	Geel Rivier	[xeəl rifir]
Yangtze	Blou Rivier	[blæu rifir]
Mekong	Mekong	[mekoŋ]
Ganges	Ganges	[xaŋəs]

Nile River	Nyl	[najl]
Congo River	Kongorivier	[kongo·rifir]
Okavango River	Okavango	[okavango]
Zambezi River	Zambezi	[sambesi]
Limpopo River	Limpopo	[limpopo]
Mississippi River	Mississippi	[mississippi]

83. Forest

forest, wood	bos	[bos]
forest (as adj)	bos-	[bos-]

thick forest	woud	[væut]
grove	boord	[boərt]
forest clearing	oopte	[oəptə]

thicket	struikgewas	[strœik·xevas]
scrubland	struikveld	[strœik·fɛlt]

footpath (troddenpath)	paadjie	[pādʒi]
gully	donga	[donxa]
tree	boom	[boəm]

| leaf | blaar | [blār] |
| leaves (foliage) | blare | [blarə] |

fall of leaves	val van die blare	[fal fan di blarə]
to fall (ab. leaves)	val	[fal]
top (of the tree)	boomtop	[boəm·top]

branch	tak	[tak]
bough	tak	[tak]
bud (on shrub, tree)	knop	[knop]
needle (of pine tree)	naald	[nālt]
fir cone	dennebol	[dɛnnə·bol]

hollow (in a tree)	holte	[holtə]
nest	nes	[nes]
burrow (animal hole)	gat	[χat]

trunk	stam	[stam]
root	wortel	[vortəl]
bark	bas	[bas]
moss	mos	[mos]

to uproot (remove trees or tree stumps)	ontwortel	[ontwortəl]
to chop down	omkap	[omkap]
to deforest (vt)	ontbos	[ontbos]
tree stump	boomstomp	[boəm·stomp]

campfire	kampvuur	[kampfɪr]
forest fire	bosbrand	[bos·brant]
to extinguish (vt)	blus	[blus]

forest ranger	boswagter	[bos·waχtər]
protection	beskerming	[beskermiŋ]
to protect (~ nature)	beskerm	[beskerm]
poacher	wildstroper	[vilt·stropər]
steel trap	slagyster	[slaχ·ajstər]

| to gather, to pick (vt) | pluk | [pluk] |
| to lose one's way | verdwaal | [ferdwāl] |

84. Natural resources

natural resources	natuurlike bronne	[natɪrlikə bronnə]
minerals	minerale	[minerale]
deposits	lae	[laə]
field (e.g. oilfield)	veld	[fɛlt]

to mine (extract)	myn	[majn]
mining (extraction)	myn	[majn]
ore	erts	[ɛrts]
mine (e.g. for coal)	myn	[majn]
shaft (mine ~)	mynskag	[majn·skaχ]
miner	mynwerker	[majn·werkər]

| gas (natural ~) | gas | [χas] |
| gas pipeline | gaspyp | [χas·pajp] |

oil (petroleum)	olie	[oli]
oil pipeline	olipypleiding	[oli·pajp·læjdiŋ]
oil well	oliebron	[oli·bron]
derrick (tower)	boortoring	[boər·toriŋ]
tanker	tenkskip	[tɛnk·skip]

sand	sand	[sant]
limestone	kalksteen	[kalksteən]
gravel	gruis	[χrœis]
peat	veengrond	[feənχront]
clay	klei	[klæj]
coal	steenkool	[steən·koəl]

iron (ore)	yster	[ajstər]
gold	goud	[χæʊt]
silver	silwer	[silwər]
nickel	nikkel	[nikkəl]
copper	koper	[kopər]

zinc	sink	[sink]
manganese	mangaan	[manχān]
mercury	kwik	[kwik]
lead	lood	[loət]

mineral	mineraal	[minerāl]
crystal	kristal	[kristal]
marble	marmer	[marmər]
uranium	uraan	[urān]

85. Weather

weather	weer	[veər]
weather forecast	weersvoorspelling	[veərs·foərspɛlliŋ]
temperature	temperatuur	[temperatɪr]
thermometer	termometer	[termometər]
barometer	barometer	[barometər]

| humid (adj) | klam | [klam] |
| humidity | vogtigheid | [foχtiχæjt] |

heat (extreme ~)	hitte	[hittə]
hot (torrid)	heet	[heət]
it's hot	dis vrekwarm	[dis frekvarm]

| it's warm | dit is warm | [dit is varm] |
| warm (moderately hot) | louwarm | [læʊvarm] |

it's cold	dis koud	[dis kæʊt]
cold (adj)	koud	[kæʊt]
sun	son	[son]
to shine (vi)	skyn	[skajn]

sunny (day)	sonnig	[sonnəχ]
to come up (vi)	opkom	[opkom]
to set (vi)	ondergaan	[ondərχān]

cloud	wolk	[volk]
cloudy (adj)	bewolk	[bevolk]
rain cloud	reënwolk	[rɛɛn·wolk]
somber (gloomy)	somber	[sombər]

rain	reën	[rɛɛn]
it's raining	dit reën	[dit rɛɛn]
rainy (~ day, weather)	reënerig	[rɛɛnerəχ]
to drizzle (vi)	motreën	[motrɛɛn]

pouring rain	stortbui	[stortbœi]
downpour	reënvlaag	[rɛɛn·flāχ]
heavy (e.g. ~ rain)	swaar	[swār]
puddle	poeletjie	[puləki]
to get wet (in rain)	nat word	[nat vort]

fog (mist)	mis	[mis]
foggy	mistig	[mistəχ]
snow	sneeu	[sniʊ]
it's snowing	dit sneeu	[dit sniʊ]

86. Severe weather. Natural disasters

thunderstorm	donderstorm	[dondər·storm]
lightning (~ strike)	weerlig	[veərləχ]
to flash (vi)	flits	[flits]

thunder	donder	[dondər]
to thunder (vi)	donder	[dondər]
it's thundering	dit donder	[dit dondər]

| hail | hael | [haəl] |
| it's hailing | dit hael | [dit haəl] |

| to flood (vt) | oorstroom | [oərstroəm] |
| flood, inundation | oorstroming | [oərstromiŋ] |

earthquake	aardbewing	[ārd·beviŋ]
tremor, quake	aardskok	[ārd·skok]
epicentre	episentrum	[ɛpisentrum]

| eruption | uitbarsting | [œitbarstiŋ] |
| lava | lawa | [lava] |

| twister, tornado | tornado | [tornadə] |
| typhoon | tifoon | [tifoən] |

hurricane	orkaan	[orkān]
storm	storm	[storm]
tsunami	tsunami	[tsunami]

cyclone	sikloon	[sikloən]
bad weather	slegte weer	[sleχtə veər]
fire (accident)	brand	[brant]
disaster	ramp	[ramp]
meteorite	meteoriet	[meteorit]

avalanche	lawine	[lavinə]
snowslide	sneeulawine	[sniʊˑlavinə]
blizzard	sneeustorm	[sniʊˑstorm]
snowstorm	sneeustorm	[sniʊˑstorm]

FAUNA

87. Mammals. Predators

predator	roofdier	[roef·dir]
tiger	tier	[tir]
lion	leeu	[liʊ]
wolf	wolf	[volf]
fox	vos	[fos]

jaguar	jaguar	[jaχuar]
leopard	luiperd	[lœipert]
cheetah	jagluiperd	[jaχ·lœipert]

black panther	swart luiperd	[swart lœipert]
puma	poema	[puma]
snow leopard	sneeuluiperd	[sniʊ·lœipert]
lynx	los	[los]

coyote	prèriewolf	[præri·volf]
jackal	jakkals	[jakkals]
hyena	hiëna	[hiɛna]

88. Wild animals

animal	dier	[dir]
beast (animal)	beest	[beəst]

squirrel	eekhoring	[eəkhoriŋ]
hedgehog	krimpvarkie	[krimpfarki]
hare	hasie	[hasi]
rabbit	konyn	[konajn]

badger	das	[das]
raccoon	wasbeer	[vasbeər]
hamster	hamster	[hamstər]
marmot	marmot	[marmot]

mole	mol	[mol]
mouse	muis	[mœis]
rat	rot	[rot]
bat	vlermuis	[fler·mœis]

ermine	hermelyn	[hermәlajn]
sable	sabel, sabeldier	[sabәl], [sabәl·dir]
marten	marter	[martәr]
weasel	wesel	[vesәl]
mink	nerts	[nerts]

| beaver | bewer | [bevər] |
| otter | otter | [ottər] |

horse	perd	[pert]
moose	eland	[ɛlant]
deer	hert	[hert]
camel	kameel	[kameəl]

bison	bison	[bison]
aurochs	wisent	[visent]
buffalo	buffel	[buffəl]

zebra	sebra, kwagga	[sebra], [kwaχχa]
antelope	wildsbok	[vilds·bok]
roe deer	reebok	[reəbok]
fallow deer	damhert	[damhert]
chamois	gems	[χems]
wild boar	wildevark	[vildə·fark]

whale	walvis	[valfis]
seal	seehond	[seə·hont]
walrus	walrus	[valrus]
fur seal	seebeer	[seə·beər]
dolphin	dolfyn	[dolfajn]

bear	beer	[beər]
polar bear	ysbeer	[ajs·beər]
panda	panda	[panda]

monkey	aap	[āp]
chimpanzee	sjimpansee	[ʃimpaŋseə]
orangutan	orangoetang	[oranχutaŋ]
gorilla	gorilla	[χorilla]
macaque	makaak	[makāk]
gibbon	gibbon	[χibbon]

elephant	olifant	[olifant]
rhinoceros	renoster	[renostər]
giraffe	kameelperd	[kameəl·pert]
hippopotamus	seekoei	[seə·kui]

| kangaroo | kangaroe | [kanχaru] |
| koala (bear) | koala | [koala] |

mongoose	muishond	[mœis·hont]
chinchilla	chinchilla, tjintjilla	[tʃin·tʃila]
skunk	stinkmuishond	[stinkmœis·hont]
porcupine	ystervark	[ajstər·fark]

89. Domestic animals

cat	kat	[kat]
tomcat	kater	[katər]
dog	hond	[hont]

horse	perd	[pert]
stallion (male horse)	hings	[hiŋs]
mare	merrie	[merri]

cow	koei	[kui]
bull	bul	[bul]
ox	os	[os]

sheep (ewe)	skaap	[skāp]
ram	ram	[ram]
goat	bok	[bok]
billy goat, he-goat	bokram	[bok·ram]

| donkey | donkie, esel | [donki], [eisəl] |
| mule | muil | [mœil] |

pig	vark	[fark]
piglet	varkie	[farki]
rabbit	konyn	[konajn]

| hen (chicken) | hoender, hen | [hundər], [hen] |
| cock | haan | [hān] |

duck	eend	[eent]
drake	mannetjieseend	[mannəkis·eent]
goose	gans	[χaŋs]

| tom turkey, gobbler | kalkoenmannetjie | [kalkun·mannəki] |
| turkey (hen) | kalkoen | [kalkun] |

domestic animals	huisdiere	[hœis·dirə]
tame (e.g. ~ hamster)	mak	[mak]
to tame (vt)	mak maak	[mak māk]
to breed (vt)	teel	[teəl]

farm	plaas	[plās]
poultry	pluimvee	[plœimfeə]
cattle	beeste	[beestə]
herd (cattle)	kudde	[kuddə]

stable	stal	[stal]
pigsty	varkstal	[fark·stal]
cowshed	koeistal	[kui·stal]
rabbit hutch	konynehok	[konajnə·hok]
hen house	hoenderhok	[hundər·hok]

90. Birds

bird	voël	[foɛl]
pigeon	duif	[dœif]
sparrow	mossie	[mossi]
tit (great tit)	mees	[meəs]
magpie	ekster	[ɛkstər]
raven	raaf	[rāf]

crow	kraai	[krāi]
jackdaw	kerkkraai	[kerk·krāi]
rook	roek	[ruk]

duck	eend	[eent]
goose	gans	[χaŋs]
pheasant	fisant	[fisant]

eagle	arend	[arɛnt]
hawk	sperwer	[sperwər]
falcon	valk	[falk]
vulture	aasvoël	[āsfoɛl]
condor (Andean ~)	kondor	[kondor]

swan	swaan	[swān]
crane	kraanvoël	[krān·foɛl]
stork	ooievaar	[ojefār]

parrot	papegaai	[papəχāi]
hummingbird	kolibrie	[kolibri]
peacock	pou	[pæʊ]

ostrich	volstruis	[folstrœis]
heron	reier	[ræjer]
flamingo	flamink	[flamink]
pelican	pelikaan	[pelikān]

| nightingale | nagtegaal | [naχteχāl] |
| swallow | swael | [swaəl] |

thrush	lyster	[lajstər]
song thrush	sanglyster	[saŋlajstər]
blackbird	merel	[merəl]

swift	windswael	[vindswaəl]
lark	lewerik	[leverik]
quail	kwartel	[kwartəl]

woodpecker	speg	[speχ]
cuckoo	koekoek	[kukuk]
owl	uil	[œil]
eagle owl	ooruil	[oərœil]
wood grouse	auerhoen	[ɔuer·hun]
black grouse	korhoen	[korhun]
partridge	patrys	[patrajs]

starling	spreeu	[spriʊ]
canary	kanarie	[kanari]
hazel grouse	bonasa hoen	[bonasa hun]

| chaffinch | gryskoppie | [χrajskoppi] |
| bullfinch | bloedvink | [bludfink] |

seagull	seemeeu	[seəmiʊ]
albatross	albatros	[albatros]
penguin	pikkewyn	[pikkəvajn]

91. Fish. Marine animals

bream	brasem	[brasem]
carp	karp	[karp]
perch	baars	[bārs]
catfish	katvis, seebaber	[katfis], [seə·babər]
pike	snoek	[snuk]
salmon	salm	[salm]
sturgeon	steur	[støər]
herring	haring	[hariŋ]
Atlantic salmon	atlantiese salm	[atlantisə salm]
mackerel	makriel	[makril]
flatfish	platvis	[platfis]
zander, pike perch	varswatersnoek	[farswatər·snuk]
cod	kabeljou	[kabeljæʊ]
tuna	tuna	[tuna]
trout	forel	[forəl]
eel	paling	[paliŋ]
electric ray	drilvis	[drilfis]
moray eel	bontpaling	[bontpaliŋ]
piranha	piranha	[piranha]
shark	haai	[hāi]
dolphin	dolfyn	[dolfajn]
whale	walvis	[valfis]
crab	krap	[krap]
jellyfish	jellievis	[jelli·fis]
octopus	seekat	[seə·kat]
starfish	seester	[seə·stər]
sea urchin	see-egel, seekastaiing	[seə-eɣel], [seə·kastajiŋ]
seahorse	seeperdjie	[seə·perdʒi]
oyster	oester	[ustər]
prawn	garnaal	[ɣarnāl]
lobster	kreef	[kreəf]
spiny lobster	seekreef	[seə·kreəf]

92. Amphibians. Reptiles

snake	slang	[slaŋ]
venomous (snake)	giftig	[ɣiftəɣ]
viper	adder	[addər]
cobra	kobra	[kobra]
python	luislang	[lœislaŋ]
boa	boa, konstriktorslang	[boa], [kɔŋstriktor·slaŋ]
grass snake	ringslang	[riŋ·slaŋ]

| rattle snake | ratelslang | [ratəl·slaŋ] |
| anaconda | anakonda | [anakonda] |

lizard	akkedis	[akkedis]
iguana	leguaan	[leχuãn]
monitor lizard	likkewaan	[likkevãn]
salamander	salamander	[salamandər]
chameleon	verkleurmannetjie	[ferkløər·manneki]
scorpion	skerpioen	[skerpiun]

turtle	skilpad	[skilpat]
frog	padda	[padda]
toad	brulpadda	[brul·padda]
crocodile	krokodil	[krokodil]

93. Insects

insect	insek	[insek]
butterfly	skoenlapper	[skunlappər]
ant	mier	[mir]
fly	vlieg	[fliχ]
mosquito	muskiet	[muskit]
beetle	kewer	[kevər]

wasp	perdeby	[perdə·baj]
bee	by	[baj]
bumblebee	hommelby	[homməl·baj]
gadfly (botfly)	perdevlieg	[pərdə·fliχ]

| spider | spinnekop | [spinnə·kop] |
| spider's web | spinnerak | [spinnə·rak] |

dragonfly	naaldekoker	[nãldə·kokər]
grasshopper	sprinkaan	[sprinkãn]
moth (night butterfly)	mot	[mot]

cockroach	kakkerlak	[kakkerlak]
tick	bosluis	[boslœis]
flea	vlooi	[floj]
midge	muggie	[muχχi]

locust	treksprinkhaan	[trek·sprinkhãn]
snail	slak	[slak]
cricket	kriek	[krik]
firefly	vuurvliegie	[fɪrfliχi]
ladybird	lieweheersbesie	[liveheərs·besi]
cockchafer	lentekewer	[lentekevər]

leech	bloedsuier	[blud·sœeiər]
caterpillar	ruspe	[ruspə]
earthworm	erdwurm	[ɛrd·vurm]
larva	larwe	[larvə]

FLORA

94. Trees

tree	boom	[boəm]
deciduous (adj)	bladwisselend	[bladwisselent]
coniferous (adj)	kegeldraend	[keχɛldraent]
evergreen (adj)	immergroen	[immərχrun]
apple tree	appelboom	[appɛl·boəm]
pear tree	peerboom	[peər·boəm]
cherry tree	kersieboom	[kersi·boəm]
sweet cherry tree	soetkersieboom	[sutkersi·boəm]
sour cherry tree	suurkersieboom	[sɪrkersi·boəm]
plum tree	pruimeboom	[prœimə·boəm]
birch	berk	[berk]
oak	eik	[æjk]
linden tree	lindeboom	[lində·boəm]
aspen	trilpopulier	[trilpopulir]
maple	esdoring	[ɛsdoriŋ]
spruce	spar	[spar]
pine	denneboom	[dɛnnə·boəm]
larch	lorkeboom	[lorkə·boəm]
fir tree	den	[den]
cedar	seder	[sedər]
poplar	populier	[populir]
rowan	lysterbessie	[lajstərbɛssi]
willow	wilger	[vilχər]
alder	els	[ɛls]
beech	beuk	[bøək]
elm	olm	[olm]
ash (tree)	esboom	[ɛs·boəm]
chestnut	kastaiing	[kastajiŋ]
magnolia	magnolia	[maχnolia]
palm tree	palm	[palm]
cypress	sipres	[sipres]
mangrove	wortelboom	[vortəl·boəm]
baobab	kremetart	[kremetart]
eucalyptus	bloekom	[blukom]
sequoia	mammoetboom	[mammut·boəm]

95. Shrubs

| bush | struik | [strœik] |
| shrub | bossie | [bossi] |

| grapevine | wingerdstok | [viŋerd·stok] |
| vineyard | wingerd | [viŋert] |

raspberry bush	framboosstruik	[framboes·strœik]
blackcurrant bush	swartbessiestruik	[swartbɛssi·strœik]
redcurrant bush	rooi aalbessiestruik	[roj ālbɛssi·strœik]
gooseberry bush	appelliefiestruik	[appɛllifi·strœik]

acacia	akasia	[akasia]
barberry	suurbessie	[sɪr·bɛssi]
jasmine	jasmyn	[jasmajn]

juniper	jenewer	[jenevər]
rosebush	roosstruik	[roes·strœik]
dog rose	hondsroos	[honds·roes]

96. Fruits. Berries

| fruit | vrug | [fruχ] |
| fruits | vrugte | [fruχtə] |

apple	appel	[appəl]
pear	peer	[peər]
plum	pruim	[prœim]

strawberry (garden ~)	aarbei	[ārbæj]
cherry	kersie	[kersi]
sour cherry	suurkersie	[sɪr·kersi]
sweet cherry	soetkersie	[sut·kersi]
grape	druif	[drœif]

raspberry	framboos	[framboes]
blackcurrant	swartbessie	[swartbɛssi]
redcurrant	rooi aalbessie	[roj ālbɛssi]
gooseberry	appelliefie	[appɛllifi]
cranberry	bosbessie	[bosbɛssi]

orange	lemoen	[lemun]
tangerine	nartjie	[narki]
pineapple	pynappel	[pajnappəl]
banana	piesang	[pisaŋ]
date	dadel	[dadəl]

lemon	suurlemoen	[sɪr·lemun]
apricot	appelkoos	[appɛlkoes]
peach	perske	[perskə]
kiwi	kiwi, kiwivrug	[kivi], [kivi·fruχ]
grapefruit	pomelo	[pomelo]

berry	bessie	[bɛssi]
berries	bessies	[bɛssis]
cowberry	pryselbessie	[prajsɛlbɛssi]
wild strawberry	wilde aarbei	[vildə ārbæj]
bilberry	bloubessie	[blæʊbɛssi]

97. Flowers. Plants

| flower | blom | [blom] |
| bouquet (of flowers) | boeket | [buket] |

rose (flower)	roos	[roəs]
tulip	tulp	[tulp]
carnation	angelier	[anχəlir]
gladiolus	swaardlelie	[swārd·leli]

cornflower	koringblom	[koriŋblom]
harebell	grasklokkie	[χras·klokki]
dandelion	perdeblom	[perdə·blom]
camomile	kamille	[kamillə]

aloe	aalwyn	[ālwajn]
cactus	kaktus	[kaktus]
rubber plant, ficus	rubberplant	[rubbər·plant]

lily	lelie	[leli]
geranium	malva	[malfa]
hyacinth	hiasint	[hiasint]

mimosa	mimosa	[mimosa]
narcissus	narsing	[narsiŋ]
nasturtium	kappertjie	[kapperki]

orchid	orgidee	[orχideə]
peony	pinksterroos	[pinkstər·roəs]
violet	viooltjie	[fioəlki]

pansy	gesiggie	[χesiχi]
forget-me-not	vergeet-my-nietjie	[ferχeət-maj-niki]
daisy	madeliefie	[madelifi]

poppy	papawer	[papavər]
hemp	hennep	[hɛnnəp]
mint	kruisement	[krœisəment]

| lily of the valley | dallelie | [dalleli] |
| snowdrop | sneeuklokkie | [sniʊ·klokki] |

nettle	brandnetel	[brant·netəl]
sorrel	veldsuring	[fɛltsuriŋ]
water lily	waterlelie	[vatər·leli]
fern	varing	[fariŋ]
lichen	korsmos	[korsmos]
greenhouse (tropical ~)	broeikas	[bruikas]

| lawn | grasperk | [χras·perk] |
| flowerbed | blombed | [blom·bet] |

plant	plant	[plant]
grass	gras	[χras]
blade of grass	grasspriet	[χras·sprit]

leaf	blaar	[blãr]
petal	kroonblaar	[kroən·blãr]
stem	stingel	[stiŋəl]
tuber	knol	[knol]

| young plant (shoot) | saailing | [sãjliŋ] |
| thorn | doring | [doriŋ] |

to blossom (vi)	bloei	[blui]
to fade, to wither	verlep	[ferlep]
smell (odour)	reuk	[røək]
to cut (flowers)	sny	[snaj]
to pick (a flower)	pluk	[pluk]

98. Cereals, grains

grain	graan	[χrãn]
cereal crops	graangewasse	[χrãn·χəwassə]
ear (of barley, etc.)	aar	[ãr]

wheat	koring	[koriŋ]
rye	rog	[roχ]
oats	hawer	[havər]
millet	gierst	[χirst]
barley	gars	[χars]

maize	mielie	[mili]
rice	rys	[rajs]
buckwheat	bokwiet	[bokwit]

pea plant	ertjie	[ɛrki]
kidney bean	nierboon	[nir·boən]
soya	soja	[soja]
lentil	lensie	[lɛŋsi]
beans (pulse crops)	boontjies	[boənkis]

COUNTRIES OF THE WORLD

99. Countries. Part 1

Afghanistan	**Afghanistan**	[afχanistan]
Albania	**Albanië**	[albaniɛ]
Argentina	**Argentinië**	[arχentiniɛ]
Armenia	**Armenië**	[armeniɛ]
Australia	**Australië**	[ɔustraliɛ]
Austria	**Oostenryk**	[oəstenrajk]
Azerbaijan	**Azerbeidjan**	[azerbæjdjan]
The Bahamas	**die Bahamas**	[di bahamas]
Bangladesh	**Bangladesj**	[bangladeʃ]
Belarus	**Belarus**	[belarus]
Belgium	**België**	[belχiɛ]
Bolivia	**Bolivië**	[boliviɛ]
Bosnia and Herzegovina	**Bosnië & Herzegowina**	[bosniɛ en hersegovina]
Brazil	**Brasilië**	[brasiliɛ]
Bulgaria	**Bulgarye**	[bulχaraje]
Cambodia	**Kambodja**	[kambodja]
Canada	**Kanada**	[kanada]
Chile	**Chili**	[tʃili]
China	**Sjina**	[ʃina]
Colombia	**Colombia, Kolombië**	[kolombia], [kolombiɛ]
Croatia	**Kroasië**	[kroasiɛ]
Cuba	**Kuba**	[kuba]
Cyprus	**Ciprus**	[siprus]
Czech Republic	**Tjeggië**	[tʃeχiɛ]
Denmark	**Denemarke**	[denemarkə]
Dominican Republic	**Dominikaanse Republiek**	[dominikãnsə republik]
Ecuador	**Ecuador**	[ɛkuador]
Egypt	**Egipte**	[ɛχiptə]
England	**Engeland**	[ɛŋəlant]
Estonia	**Estland**	[ɛstlant]
Finland	**Finland**	[finlant]
France	**Frankryk**	[frankrajk]
French Polynesia	**Frans-Polinesië**	[fraŋs-polinesiɛ]
Georgia	**Georgië**	[χeorχiɛ]
Germany	**Duitsland**	[dœitslant]
Ghana	**Ghana**	[χana]
Great Britain	**Groot-Brittanje**	[χroət-brittanje]
Greece	**Griekeland**	[χrikəlant]
Haiti	**Haïti**	[haïti]
Hungary	**Hongarye**	[honχaraje]

100. Countries. Part 2

Iceland	Ysland	[ajslant]
India	Indië	[indiɛ]
Indonesia	Indonesië	[indonesiɛ]
Iran	Iran	[iran]
Iraq	Irak	[irak]
Ireland	Ierland	[irlant]
Israel	Israel	[israəl]
Italy	Italië	[italiɛ]

Jamaica	Jamaika	[jamajka]
Japan	Japan	[japan]
Jordan	Jordanië	[jordaniɛ]
Kazakhstan	Kazakstan	[kasakstan]
Kenya	Kenia	[kenia]
Kirghizia	Kirgisië	[kirχisiɛ]
Kuwait	Kuwait	[kuvajt]

Laos	Laos	[laos]
Latvia	Letland	[letlant]
Lebanon	Libanon	[libanon]
Libya	Libië	[libiɛ]
Liechtenstein	Lichtenstein	[liχtɛŋstejn]
Lithuania	Litoue	[litæʋə]
Luxembourg	Luksemburg	[luksemburχ]

Macedonia (Republic of ~)	Masedonië	[masedoniɛ]
Madagascar	Madagaskar	[madaχaskar]
Malaysia	Maleisië	[malæjsiɛ]
Malta	Malta	[malta]
Mexico	Meksiko	[meksiko]

Moldova, Moldavia	Moldawië	[moldaviɛ]
Monaco	Monako	[monako]
Mongolia	Mongolië	[monχoliɛ]
Montenegro	Montenegro	[montenegro]
Morocco	Marokko	[marokko]
Myanmar	Myanmar	[mjanmar]

Namibia	Namibië	[namibiɛ]
Nepal	Nepal	[nepal]
Netherlands	Nederland	[nedərlant]
New Zealand	Nieu-Seeland	[niu-seəlant]
North Korea	Noord-Korea	[noərd-korea]
Norway	Noorweë	[noərweɛ]

101. Countries. Part 3

Pakistan	Pakistan	[pakistan]
Palestine	Palestina	[palestina]
Panama	Panama	[panama]
Paraguay	Paraguay	[paragwaj]

Peru	Peru	[peru]
Poland	Pole	[polə]
Portugal	Portugal	[portuχal]
Romania	Roemenië	[rumenιɛ]
Russia	Rusland	[ruslant]

Saudi Arabia	Saoedi-Arabië	[saudi-arabiɛ]
Scotland	Skotland	[skotlant]
Senegal	Senegal	[seneχal]
Serbia	Serwië	[serwiɛ]
Slovakia	Slowakye	[slovakaje]
Slovenia	Slovenië	[slofeniɛ]

South Africa	Suid-Afrika	[sœid-afrika]
South Korea	Suid-Korea	[sœid-korea]
Spain	Spanje	[spanjə]
Suriname	Suriname	[surinamə]
Sweden	Swede	[swedə]
Switzerland	Switserland	[switsərlant]
Syria	Sirië	[siriɛ]

Taiwan	Taiwan	[tajvan]
Tajikistan	Tadjikistan	[tadʒikistan]
Tanzania	Tanzanië	[tansaniɛ]
Tasmania	Tasmanië	[tasmaniɛ]
Thailand	Thailand	[tajlant]
Tunisia	Tunisië	[tunisiɛ]
Turkey	Turkye	[turkaje]
Turkmenistan	Turkmenistan	[turkmenistan]

Ukraine	Oekraïne	[ukraïnə]
United Arab Emirates	Verenigde Arabiese Emirate	[fereniχdə arabisə emiratə]
United States of America	Verenigde State van Amerika	[fereniχdə statə fan amerika]
Uruguay	Uruguay	[urugwaj]
Uzbekistan	Oezbekistan	[uzbekistan]

Vatican	Vatikaan	[fatikãn]
Venezuela	Venezuela	[fenesuela]
Vietnam	Viëtnam	[viɛtnam]
Zanzibar	Zanzibar	[zanzibar]

www.ingramcontent.com/pod-product-compliance
Lightning Source LLC
Chambersburg PA
CBHW070832050426
42452CB00011B/2250